# VEGETARIAN COOKING

HAMLYN
*new*
COOKERY

# VEGETARIAN COOKING

## LOUISE PICKFORD

First published in Great Britain in 1994
by Hamlyn
an imprint of Reed Consumer Books Limited
Michelin House, 81 Fulham Road, London SW3 6RB
and Auckland, Melbourne, Singapore and Toronto

ISBN 0 600 58081 4

A CIP catalogue record for this book is available from the
British Library

Printed in the UK by Butler and Tanner


ACKNOWLEDGEMENTS

Art Director Jacqui Small
Art Editor Penny Stock
Designers Clare White and Barbara Zuniga
Commissioning Editor Nicky Hill
Editors Jeni Fleetwood and Sasha Judelson
Production Controller Melaine Frantz
Photographer Gus Filgate
Photo Direction Cherry Ramseyer
Home Economist Louise Pickford
Stylist Penny Markham

*NOTES*

Both metric and imperial measurements have been given
in all recipes. Use one set of measurements only and not a
mixture of both.

Standard level spoon measurements are used in all recipes.
1 tablespoon = one 15 ml spoon
1 teaspoon = one 5 ml spoon

Eggs should be size 3 unless otherwise stated.

Milk should be full fat unless otherwise stated.

Pepper should be freshly ground black pepper unless
otherwise stated.

Fresh herbs should be used unless otherwise stated. If
unavailable use dried herbs as an alternative but halve
the quantities stated.

Ovens should be preheated to the specified temperature
- if using a fan assisted oven, follow the manufacturer's
instructions for adjusting the time and the temperature.

# CONTENTS

# INTRODUCTION

It may surprise some people to discover that vegetarianism is not a modern invention, it has in fact been with us for thousands of years. It seems strange then that until recently vegetarians have often been considered cranks. Thankfully, this attitude is becoming a thing of the past, due in part to the increase in vegetarians, who now make up approximately seven per cent of the population.

As we move into the mid-1990s the emphasis on looking and feeling healthy becomes ever stronger, and diet and health become synonymous. With concern that the consumption of red meat and animal fats are a contributing factor to the increasing rate of heart disease, a vegetarian diet appears particularly appealing.

This book offers a comprehensive guide to the preparation and cooking of vegetables, rice, pasta, grains, beans, fruits, eggs and cheeses for vegetarians and carnivores alike who enjoy meals without meat and are looking for a diet which will help provide a healthier body. The recipes are divided into chapters in order to help plan meals and menus. I have drawn on many influences in putting together this collection of recipes. I hope to have been as comprehensive as possible for vegetarian and carnivore alike.

## A HEALTHY OPTION

It is wrong to assume that a meat-free diet guarantees better health; a balance of vital nutrients is required to maintain good health. Vegetarians often wrongly supplement a lack of meat in their diet with an excess of dairy and other products such as milk, eggs and cheese, themselves high in saturated fats and cholesterol.

In order to perform at their best our bodies need a combination of the following – protein, carbohydrates, vitamins, minerals, and fats.

### PROTEIN

Beans, grains, nuts, soya products (tofu), milk, eggs and cheese as well as many vegetables, contain valuable sources of protein needed to ensure the growth of all our body cells. Although our bodies manufacture certain proteins (amino-acids) the essential amino-acids we need can only be found in food sources. It is mainly animal fats that contain these essential amino-acids, with soya products being the only exception. However, by food combining (eating certain foods together) we can obtain all the essentials which are lacking in individual foods. A good example of foods that combine together is pasta with chickpeas, rice and nuts, and bran and yogurt.

### CARBOHYDRATES

The confusion of the two types of carbohydrates (simple and complex) led in the past to all carbohydrates being given a bad name. Starchy foods such as cereals, whole grains, fruits, vegetables, potatoes and pastas, which are the complex carbohydrates, also contain important minerals and vitamins and are therefore a vital part of a healthy diet. Avoid simple carbohydrates (also called free sugars), as they have little real food value and are sometimes known as empty calories.

### VITAMINS

Vitamins are essential for the body to function properly, with vitamins A, C and E being particularly important for disease prevention and the B vitamins for a healthy nervous system and the release of energy from all foods as we digest them. They come in two types, and are fat- or water-soluble. The liver stores the fat-soluble vitamins A, D, E and K which are found in fatty foods. As the water-soluble vitamins C and B dissolve in water they cannot be stored and so must be supplemented. It is important for vegetarians and vegans to ensure they are getting sufficient of these vitamins, especially vitamin B12, found mainly in animal products.

MINERALS

The body cannot make minerals and these must be provided by foods. Iron, calcium and zinc are three minerals that vegetarians and vegans may need to supplement, while other important minerals should be available through a good varied diet. Iron is important in the production of haemoglobin in blood and can be found in green vegetables, nuts, some cereals and some dried fruits. Calcium is necessary for healthy bones, tissues and teeth and is found in dairy products, wheat, dried fruits, nuts and green vegetables. Zinc obtained from vegetable rather than animal products is harder for the body to absorb so, vegetarians may be at greater risk of zinc deficiency than carnivores. Zinc is present in grains, nuts, pulses and cereals.

FATS

These should not be totally ignored in a balanced diet as they give the body energy, and also help to keep us warm in the winter. However, saturated fats – those which are high in cholesterol – found in animal products should be avoided, wherever it is possible to do so. Vegetable oils such as sunflower and olive oil are unsaturated and should be used instead of butter and other saturated fats. Fatty foods tend to fill us up more quickly, but by substituting starchy foods for these fatty foods we can satisfy our hunger and also be healthier at the same time.

## GLOSSARY OF INGREDIENTS

STORE CUPBOARD

**Arborio** The Italian rice used in making risottos. It is similar in shape and texture to pudding rice, but never quite softens in the middle.

**Balsamic vinegar** Italian vinegar that has been aged for anything up to 20 years in oak casks (much like some red wines). It is dark, with an intense, slightly sweet flavour.

**Buckwheat** Small, triangular-shaped grain, milled into either flour or grains. The roasted variety has a deeper flavour. It is a staple food of Russia and Eastern Europe and is served as an accompaniment.

**Bulgar wheat** Cracked wheat that has been partially processed. Sometimes sold as cracked wheat or pourgouri, and is used extensively in Middle Eastern cooking where it is eaten in the same way as rice.

**Capers** Small buds of a flowering shrub grown in the Mediterranean. Normally pickled in brine or salted, they should be washed and dried before use.

**Cassis** A fruit liqueur or syrup made from blackcurrants; usually added to wine or champagne to serve as a refreshing aperitif.

**Chilli Sauce** This can be found in many supermarkets and Oriental stores. To make your own put 1 tablespoon of soft brown sugar together with 2 tablespoons of dark-soy sauce, 1 tablespoon of lime juice and 1 red chilli, deseeded and chopped, in a small saucepan and heat until the sugar dissolves.

**Coconut milk** Available in cans from ethnic stores or larger supermarkets.

**Couscous** Actually a type of pasta although it is generally treated like a grain and is pre-soaked before cooking to soften it. Used in North African and Middle Eastern cooking.

**Curry paste** Available in jars, as mild, medium and hot.

**Dried ceps** Dried mushrooms that need reconstituting in boiling water for at least 20 minutes before using. Also known as *porcini,* their Italian name. They are available from specialist food stores and delicatessens. A little go a long way.

**Dulse seaweed** Available dried from good health food stores, this seaweed is dark purple/red in colour. It has a strong flavour and is similar to purple *nori.*

**Fast-acting yeast** Dried yeast, sometimes called easy-blend yeast, it can be added directly to the flour, it often only needs one rising (see individual packet) as it contains an enzyme that speeds up the rising process of fresh or compressed yeast.

**Fermented black beans** Tiny black beans available in both packets and cans from Oriental stores. Soak them in cold water for 30 minutes to remove excess saltiness.

**Fresh yeast** Buy fresh yeast if possible when making bread, for superior flavour. Otherwise use 25 g/1 oz dried or 1 teaspoon fast-acting yeast instead of 15 g/½ oz fresh yeast.

**Garam masala** A ready-made spice powder made up of several different Indian spices.

**Kalamata olives** Greek olives that are pointed at one end and are a purple-brown colour.

**Millet** A small pinhead grain with a nutty flavour. Needs no soaking if it is to be cooked through.

**Nuts** Should be used up quickly as they do not keep well.

**Oils** Olive oil should be extra virgin unless recipe states otherwise. Use sunflower oil or a good quality vegetable oil for deep-frying. Nut oils do not keep well and should be stored in a cool dark place.

**Passata** Sieved tomatoes, available from supermarkets.

**Polenta** The Italian name for corn-meal. Used to make a porridge-like gruel or set and grilled in triangles. Quick polenta is best as it takes only a few minutes to cook.

**Rosewater** Water flavoured with the essence of rose petals and added to sweet dishes for an exotic flavour. Used mainly in Turkish, Greek and Middle Eastern cooking.

**Sun-dried tomatoes** Available in dried form but I prefer those packed in oil.

**Tahini paste** A purée of sesame seeds plain or toasted, used extensively in Middle Eastern cooking. Oriental sesame paste is different so is best bought from Oriental stores.

**Tamari soy sauce** This is a slightly thicker, sweeter soy sauce and is available in some supermarkets and Oriental stores.

FRESH INGREDIENTS

**Bouquet garni** A bundle of fresh herbs and whole peppercorns used to flavour stocks and stews. Usually wrapped in a muslin bag which is removed after cooking.

**Butternut squash** A winter squash, but is often available all year round.

It has a smooth, thick, pale orange skin and is club-shaped.

**Celeriac** A root vegetable with greenish knobbly skin. It is like celery in flavour, with a creamy texture once cooked.

**Coriander root** Roots that are still attached to bunches of coriander are used as an aromatic in Thai cooking.

**Fennel fronds** The wispy leaves of the fennel bulb, which are occasionally sold still attached to the bulb. Dill is an alternative.

**Jerusalem artichoke** A tuber, unrelated to the globe artichoke. Small and knobbly with a beige skin, it has a delicious nutty, slightly peppery flavour, and is good in soups, stews or roasted.

**Kaffir lime leaves** A variety of lime leaf used in Far Eastern cooking which can sometimes be found fresh in the larger supermarkets. They are also available in Oriental stores.

**Lemon grass** A South-East Asian

### MAKING RAVIOLI

**1** *Put a good spoonful of filling per ravioli parcel on the bottom sheet of pasta.*

**2** *Lay a second sheet of pasta over the top and then press down firmly around the filling mound*

**3** *Cut into ravioli rounds with a stamp or into squares with a sharp knife. (See page 34 for a ravioli recipe.)*

**MAKING FLAKY PASTRY**
*(See page 75 for the basic recipe.)*
**1** *Dot the butter over ⅔ of the dough.*

**2** *Fold the uncovered third of dough over the covered dough and the remaining dough back over that.*

**3** *Seal the edges firmly with a rolling pin, turn the dough once to the left and roll out to an oblong.*

ingredient that has an aromatic lemon flavour. Available in some supermarkets or Oriental stores, it looks like a thick stalk of grass. It is fibrous and is often used as a flavouring, discarded after cooking.

**Tomatoes** Deep red tomatoes with a firm texture are best if available. If the tomatoes are still green, leave them in the sun or a warm place for a few days to ripen. Cherry tomatoes can be red, orange or yellow and are sweeter in flavour. Plum tomatoes are Italian, they are good for cooking, and available canned.

DAIRY/FRESH INGREDIENTS

**Cheese** Vegetarians should always look for the 'V' symbol on cheese to ensure that it is made with vegetable rennet. Not all cheeses are available with vegetable rennet. Feta, Cheddar, Cheshire, Red Leicester, Dolcelatte and many goat's cheeses are widely available as suitable for vegetarians.

**Creamed coconut** Coconut that has been compressed into a block and is sold in a packet. It should be kept chilled once opened.

**Crème fraîche** A French lightly soured cream, similar in taste to our soured cream.

**Egg Glaze** A really effective glaze for pastry. To make: beat 1 egg until completely combined then beat in 2 tablespoons of water or milk and a pinch of salt.

**Filo pastry** The paper-thin sheets of pastry used in Greek, Turkish and Middle Eastern cooking. Available both fresh and frozen in various sheet sizes. I tend to buy the larger sheets, to be on the safe side.

**Fromage frais** A fresh curd cheese made from pasteurized cows' milk. It has a similar texture to thick yogurt and can be used as a low-fat alternative to cream.

**Mascarpone** An Italian full-fat cream cheese made from cows' milk. Eaten with fruit or used in savoury dishes.

**Mozzarella** The Italian full-fat soft cheese used in pizzas. It is made without rennet, and is therefore quite suitable for vegetarians. There are a number of types, the best is buffaloes' milk mozzarella, which has a far superior texture and flavour although it is considerably more expensive than cows' milk mozzarella.

**Olive Paste** Widely available but check the ingredients list as not all are suitable for vegetarians. To make your own put 125 g/4 oz stoned black olives, 15 g/½ oz basil leaves and 15 g/½ oz of drained capers in a blender with 4 tablespoons of extra virgin olive oil and process to make a smooth paste.

**Ricotta** An Italian curd cheese with a deliciously mild taste and texture. Suitable for both sweet and savoury dishes, and often associated with pasta dishes and gnocchi.

**Vegetable suet** A suet made from palm and sunflower oils which is suitable for vegetarians.

## *Mexican Soup with Avocado Salsa*

2 tablespoons sunflower oil
1 large onion, chopped
2 garlic cloves, crushed
2 teaspoons ground coriander
1 teaspoon ground cumin
1 red pepper, cored, deseeded and diced
2 red chillies, deseeded and chopped
1 x 400 g/14 oz can red kidney beans
750 ml/1¼ pints tomato juice
1-2 tablespoons chilli sauce (to taste)
25 g/1 oz tortilla chips, crushed

AVOCADO SALSA:
1 small ripe avocado
4 spring onions, chopped finely
1 tablespoon lemon juice
1 tablespoon chopped fresh coriander
salt and pepper
extra tortilla chips, to garnish

**1** Heat the oil in a large saucepan, add the onion, garlic, spices, pepper and chillies and fry gently for 10 minutes. Add all the remaining ingredients except the tortilla chips, bring to the boil, cover and simmer gently for 30 minutes.

**2** Meanwhile, make the avocado salsa. Peel, stone and finely dice the avocado and combine with the remaining ingredients, seasoning to taste, cover and set aside.

**3** Process the soup in a liquidizer with the tortilla chips until smooth, return to the pan, season to taste and heat through. Spoon into bowls and serve at once topped with the avocado salsa and extra tortilla chips.

**Serves 6**
Preparation time: 30 minutes
Cooking time: 45 minutes

# Creamy Mushroom and Chestnut Soup

*A wonderfully rich and creamy soup that is sieved after liquidizing to give it a smooth texture.*

15 g/½ oz dried ceps
150 ml/¼ pint boiling water
25 g/1 oz butter
4 shallots, sliced
1 garlic clove, crushed
1 tablespoon chopped fresh thyme
500 g/1 lb brown cap mushrooms
75 ml/3 fl oz Madeira or sweet sherry
175 g/6 oz cooked canned chestnuts or
    unsweetened chestnut purée
450 ml/¾ pint Vegetable Stock (see
    page 126)
150 ml/¼ pint milk
4 tablespoons single cream (optional)
salt and pepper
chopped fresh chives and chive sprigs,
    to garnish

**1** Put the dried ceps into a small bowl and pour over the boiling water. Set aside to soak for 30 minutes. Drain, reserving the liquid.
**2** Melt the butter in a saucepan and add the shallots, garlic and thyme, fry gently for 5 minutes. Add all the mushrooms and stir-fry over a medium heat for 4-5 minutes until browned. Pour in the Madeira and boil rapidly for 3 minutes.

**3** Add the chestnuts, stock, cep liquid and milk, bring to the boil, cover and simmer gently for 25 minutes. Process the soup in a liquidizer until smooth and pass through a fine sieve back into the pan. Reheat until the soup reaches boiling point.
**4** Transfer to serving bowls, swirl in the cream if using and garnish with the chives.

**Serves 4**
Preparation time: 15 minutes, plus 30 minutes soaking
Cooking time: 35-40 minutes

## Onion and Barley Soup with Grilled Cheese Toasts

*Pearl barley needs no pre-soaking and adds a nutty bite to this delicious variation of French onion soup.*

2 tablespoons extra virgin olive oil
1 kg/2 lb onions, sliced thinly
2 garlic cloves, crushed
1 teaspoon sugar
1 teaspoon salt
2 tablespoons chopped fresh sage
150 ml/¼ pint red wine
1.2 litres/2 pints Vegetable Stock (see page 126)
50 g/2 oz pearl barley, rinsed
TOPPING:
8 thin slices French bread
125 g/4 oz vegetarian Cheddar cheese, grated
salt and pepper

**1** Heat the oil in a large saucepan, add the onions and garlic and cook over a medium heat for 20 minutes. Add the sugar, salt and sage and cook for a further 5 minutes until the onions are caramelized.
**2** Add the wine to the pan and boil rapidly for 3 minutes, then add the stock and barley. Return to the boil, cover and simmer gently for 35-40 minutes until the barley is tender. Season to taste.
**3** Lightly toast the sliced bread on each side. Spoon the soup into individual flameproof bowls and place 2 slices of toast on top of each serving. Sprinkle over the cheese and place under a preheated grill for 2-3 minutes until the cheese is melted and golden. Serve at once.

**Serves 4**
Preparation time: 15 minutes
Cooking time: 1 hour

# Vegetable Mulligatawny

*A classic Indian soup, delicately spiced. Lemon juice added to each portion before serving gives the soup an interesting kick.*

2 teaspoons coriander seeds
1 teaspoon cumin seeds
1 teaspoon fenugreek seeds
1 small dried red chilli, deseeded
  and crushed
2 tablespoons sunflower oil
1 large onion, chopped
1 garlic clove, crushed
1 teaspoon grated root ginger
1 potato, diced
175 g/6 oz red lentils, rinsed
900 ml/1½ pints Vegetable Stock (see
  page 126)
300 ml/½ pint tomato juice
1 tablespoon lemon juice
salt and pepper

**1** Dry fry the whole spices and chilli in a small frying pan until they start to pop and turn golden. Transfer to a grinder and blend to form a fine powder.
**2** Heat the oil in a saucepan and fry the onion, garlic and ginger for 5 minutes. Add the potato and ground spices and fry for a further 5 minutes.
**3** Stir in the lentils and add the stock and tomato juice. Bring to the boil, cover and cook for 30 minutes.
Add the lemon juice, taste and adjust the seasonings and serve at once.

**Serves 4**
Preparation time: 20 minutes
Cooking time: 40 minutes

VARIATION

# Spiced Carrot and Lentil Soup

2 tablespoons extra virgin olive oil
1 large onion, chopped
2 garlic cloves, crushed
375 g/12 oz carrots, chopped
1 x 400 g/14 oz can green lentils
2 teaspoons ground coriander
1 teaspoon ground cumin
1 tablespoon chopped fresh thyme
1 litre/1¾ pints vegetable stock
  (see page 126)
1 x 400 g/14 oz can chopped
  tomatoes
2 teaspoons lemon juice

**1** Heat the oil in a pan, add onion, garlic and carrots, fry for 10 minutes.
**2** Add the drained lentils, spices and thyme and stir-fry for 1 minute.
**3** Stir in the stock, tomatoes and lemon juice, bring to the boil, cover and simmer for 20 minutes. Process the soup in a blender until smooth, return to the pan and warm through.
**4** Serve the soup in individual bowls.

**Serves 6**
Preparation time: 15 minutes
Cooking time: 40 minutes

## *Celeriac Bisque*

**50 g/2 oz butter**
**1 leek, trimmed, cleaned and sliced**
**2 celery sticks, sliced**
**2 teaspoons mustard seeds**
**500 g/1 lb celeriac, chopped**
**150 ml/¼ pint dry cider or pear juice**
**900 ml/1½ pints Vegetable Stock (see**
  **page 126)**
**3 ripe pears, peeled, cored and**
  **chopped**
**50 g/2 oz walnut pieces, toasted and**
  **chopped**
**salt and pepper**

**1** Melt 40 g/1½ oz of the butter in a saucepan, add the leek, celery and mustard seeds and fry for 5 minutes until lightly golden. Stir in the celeriac and cook for a further 10 minutes.

**2** Pour in the cider or pear juice, bring to the boil and boil rapidly for 3 minutes. Add the stock, bring to the boil, cover and simmer for 20 minutes.

**3** Fry the chopped pears in the remaining butter for 3-4 minutes until golden. Add to the soup, reserving a few for garnish, with half the walnuts and cook for a further 10 minutes.

**4** Process the soup in a blender until smooth, return to the pan, season to taste and heat through for 5 minutes. Serve at once, topped with the reserved pears and walnuts.

**Serves 6**
Preparation time: 25 minutes, plus making stock
Cooking time: 45 minutes

# Suzanne's Oven-baked Soup

*Named after a close friend and very imaginative cook, this rich and creamy soup is baked in the oven, puréed with hot vegetable stock, and then returned to the oven to heat through. Roasting the vegetables in a hot oven brings out their natural sweetness, giving a wonderful depth of flavour to a dish, and makes this one of the tastiest soups I have eaten.*

1 onion, chopped roughly

2 garlic cloves

2 large carrots, sliced thickly

1 leek, trimmed, cleaned and thickly
   sliced

1 large parsnip, cubed

175 g/6 oz swede, cubed

4 tablespoons extra virgin olive oil

2 teaspoons clear honey

4 thyme sprigs

4 rosemary sprigs

2 bay leaves

4 ripe tomatoes, quartered

1.2 litres/2 pints Vegetable Stock (see
   page 126)

salt and pepper

**1** Toss the vegetables with the oil and honey and place in a roasting pan. Add the herbs and bay leaves and transfer to a preheated oven, 200°C (400°F), Gas Mark 6. Roast for about 50-60 minutes until all the vegetables are golden and tender. Add the tomatoes half-way through cooking. Lower the temperature to 190°C (375°F), Gas Mark 5.

**2** Discard the herbs and transfer the vegetables to a blender. Add half the stock and process until smooth, then blend in the remaining stock.

**3** Transfer the soup to a casserole, season to taste and bake for 20 minutes or until heated through. Serve with grilled bread and garlic sauce (see page 94).

**Serves 4**
Preparation time: 15 minutes,
Cooking time: 1¼ hours
Oven temperature: 200°C (400°F),
Gas Mark 6, then 190°C( 375°F),
Gas Mark 5

# Cauliflower, Coriander and Coconut Soup

*This recipe is based on a delicious soup served at one of my favourite Thai restaurants. The authentic flavour comes from the lemon grass, Kaffir lime leaves and ginger. Both lemon grass and lime leaves are now available in most supermarkets, which is great news for fans of Far Eastern cuisine.*

2 stalks lemon grass, chopped roughly
4 slices root ginger
4 kaffir lime leaves, bruised
2 coriander sprigs, bruised
900 ml/1½ pints Vegetable Stock (see page 126)
2 tablespoons sunflower oil
1 onion, sliced thinly
2 garlic cloves, chopped
1 teaspoon grated root ginger
1 red chilli, deseeded and sliced

1 teaspoon ground turmeric
1 cauliflower, trimmed and divided into small florets
1 x 400 g/14 oz can coconut milk
2 tablespoons chopped fresh coriander
1 tablespoon lemon juice
salt and pepper
GARNISH:
sesame oil
coriander leaves

**1** Place the lemon grass, sliced ginger, lime leaves, coriander stalks and vegetable stock in a saucepan. Bring to the boil, cover, and simmer over a gentle heat for 30 minutes.
**2** Heat the oil in a large saucepan, add the onion, chopped garlic, grated ginger and chilli and fry for 5 minutes until lightly golden. Add the turmeric and cauliflower and fry for a further 5 minutes.
**3** Strain the lemon grass stock and add to the cauliflower mixture. Stir in the coconut milk and coriander, bring to the boil and simmer very gently for 15-20 minutes until the cauliflower is cooked through. Add the lemon juice, season to taste and serve each portion of soup garnished with a drizzle of sesame oil and a few coriander leaves.

**Serves 4**
Preparation time: 20 minutes
Cooking time: 55-60 minutes

VARIATION

# Callalo Soup

25 g/1 oz butter
1 large onion, thinly sliced
2 garlic cloves, chopped
2 green chillies, deseeded and chopped
2 medium sweet potatoes, diced
¼ teaspoon ground allspice
500 g/1 lb fresh spinach, shredded
600 ml/1 pint Vegetable Stock (see page 126)
1 x 400 g/14 oz can coconut milk
1 tablespoon chopped fresh parsley
1 tablespoon chopped fresh coriander
salt and pepper
GARNISH:
1 tablespoon chopped fresh parsley
1 tablespoon chopped fresh coriander

**1** Melt the butter in a saucepan and fry the onion, garlic and chillies for 5 minutes, add the potatoes and allspice and fry for a further 5 minutes.
**2** Stir in the spinach, stock, coconut milk and herbs, bring to the boil, cover and simmer gently for 20 minutes until the vegetables are tender. Season to taste and serve hot, garnished with chopped parsley and coriander.

**Serves 6**
Preparation time: 15 minutes, plus making stock
Cooking time: 30 minutes

## Potato Cakes with Mushroom and Soured Cream Sauce

*These little potato cakes or rostis provide a lovely crispy base for the creamy mushrooms.*

**375 g/12 oz waxy potatoes**
**½ small onion, sliced very thinly**
**1 tablespoon chopped fresh dill**
**½ teaspoon salt**
**15 g/½ oz self-raising flour**
**1 egg, beaten**
**vegetable oil, for frying**
SAUCE:
**25 g/1 oz butter**
**2 shallots, chopped**
**1 garlic clove, crushed**
**375 g/12 oz button mushrooms**
**2 tablespoons chopped fresh dill**
**6 tablespoons soured cream**
**2 teaspoons creamed horseradish**
**salt and pepper**
**dill sprigs to garnish**

**1** Grate the potatoes very finely and squeeze out excess liquid. Place in a bowl and stir in the onion, dill, salt and flour. Stir the egg into the potato mixture until evenly combined.
**2** Heat 1 cm/½ inch oil in a large non-stick frying pan. Divide the potato mixture into 8 cakes and fry in batches, pressing the cakes flat, for 3-4 minutes on each side until golden. Drain the potato cakes on paper towels and keep warm.
**3** Melt the butter in a pan and fry the shallots and garlic for 5 minutes. Add the mushrooms and stir-fry over a medium heat for 5-6 minutes until golden and tender. Remove from the heat and stir in the dill, soured cream, horseradish and seasoning.
**4** Serve the potato cakes topped with mushroom sauce and dill sprigs.

**Serves 4**
Preparation time: 20 minutes
Cooking time: 10-12 minutes

## Chickpea, Spinach and Pasta Soup

2 tablespoons extra virgin olive oil
2 garlic cloves, crushed
1 onion, chopped
1 tablespoon chopped fresh rosemary
2 x 400 g/14 oz cans chickpeas with
 liquid

1.2 litres/2 pints Vegetable Stock (see
 page 126)
75 g/3 oz small pasta shapes
125 g/4 oz spinach leaves,
 shredded
salt and pepper
TO SERVE:
freshly grated nutmeg
croûtons (see below right)
freshly grated vegetarian
 Parmesan cheese

**1** Heat the oil in a large saucepan and fry the garlic, onion and rosemary for 5 minutes until softened but not golden. Add the chickpeas with their liquid and the stock, bring to the boil, cover and simmer for 30 minutes. Add the pasta, return to the boil and simmer for 6-8 minutes.
**2** Stir in the spinach and continue cooking for a further 5 minutes until both the pasta and spinach are tender. Season to taste and serve at once topped with nutmeg, croûtons and grated Parmesan.

**Serves 6**
Preparation time: 10 minutes
Cooking time: 45 minutes

## Croûtons

Remove the crusts from 4 thick slices of day-old white bread. Cut all of the bread into cubes. Heat 4 tablespoons of olive oil in a frying pan. When the oil is hot add the bread. Stir-fry for 2-3 minutes until the bread cubes are golden and crisp on all sides. Remove the croûtons from the pan with a slotted spoon and drain thoroughly on paper towels to remove any excess of oil.

**Serves 6**
Preparation time: 2 minutes
Cooking time: 2-3 minutes

# Courgette Fritters with Tzatziki

*The polenta added to the flour coating on these thinly sliced courgettes remains very crispy once cooked. The extra bite is quite delicious. Use half Greek yogurt and half natural yogurt for a more creamy tzatziki. If wished the fritters can be made in advance and reheated in a hot oven, 200°C (400°F), Gas Mark 6, for 10 minutes until crisped up.*

500 g/1 lb courgettes
25 g/1 oz polenta
25 g/1 oz plain flour
1 egg, lightly beaten
vegetable oil, for deep frying
salt and pepper

TZATZIKI:
125 g/4 oz natural yogurt
1 garlic clove, crushed
1 tablespoon chopped fresh mint
125 g/4 oz cucumber, peeled, grated and squeezed dry

**1** First make the tzatziki: place all the ingredients in a small bowl and stir well until evenly combined. Set aside for 30 minutes for the flavours to infuse.
**2** Cut the courgettes into thin slices about 5 mm/¼ inch thick. Mix the polenta and flour in a large bowl with plenty of salt and pepper. Dip the courgettes, firstly into the egg and then into the polenta to coat evenly.
**3** Put about 10 cm/4 inches of oil in a deep, heavy-bottomed saucepan and heat to 180-190°C/350-375°F, or until a cube of bread browns in 30 seconds. Fry the courgette slices in batches for 2-3 minutes until crisp and golden. Drain on paper towels and serve hot with the tzatziki to dip.

**Serves 4**
Preparation time: 10 minutes plus 30 minutes chilling
Cooking time: 2-3 minutes

VARIATION

# Fried Tomato Slices in Polenta

1kg/2 lb firm plum tomatoes
25g/1 oz polenta
15g/½ oz plain flour
1 tablespoon chopped fresh basil
salt and pepper
vegetable oil, for frying
tzatziki, to serve (see left)

**1** Cut the tomatoes lengthways into thick slices. Mix the polenta, flour, basil and salt and pepper until combined. Dip in the tomato slices to coat well on both sides.
**2** Heat a little oil in a large non-stick frying pan and fry the tomato slices, in batches for 1 minute on each side until crisp and golden.
**3** Drain on paper towels and keep warm while frying the remaining tomatoes. Serve hot with the tzatziki or a little crème fraîche.

**Serves 4**
Preparation time: 5 minutes
Cooking time: 2-3 minutes

# Glazed Mushroom and Tofu Kebabs

300 g/10 oz tofu (bean curd), evenly
   cubed
16 large button mushrooms, wiped
2 tablespoons sesame oil
6 tablespoons Tamari soy sauce
4 tablespoons red wine vinegar
2 teaspoons grated root ginger
2 garlic cloves, crushed

2 tablespoons clear honey
4 tablespoons water
1 quantity Chilli Sauce (see page 7)
PEANUT SAUCE:
1 tablespoon sunflower oil
1 garlic clove, crushed
1 red chilli, deseeded and chopped
   finely
4 tablespoons crunchy peanut butter
1 tablespoon dark soy sauce
1 tablespoon lime juice
15 g/½ oz creamed coconut

**1** Thread the tofu and mushrooms alternately on to 8 pre-soaked bamboo skewers. Combine the flavourings, honey and water in a small pan and bring to the boil. Boil rapidly until the sauce is thick and glossy and reduced by half. Leave to cool slightly.

**2** Make the chilli sauce according to the recipe on page 7.

**3** Make the peanut sauce. Heat the oil in a small saucepan and gently fry the garlic and chilli for 3 minutes. Gradually stir in the remaining ingredients. Bring slowly to the boil, stirring constantly, and add enough boiling water to make a smooth pouring sauce. Cover the surface with clingfilm and keep warm.

**4** Transfer the kebabs to a hot grill, brush all over with the glaze and cook for 8-10 minutes, turning and basting frequently, until golden and tender. Serve the kebabs hot with the 2 sauces, to dip. Accompany with rice cubes and shredded cucumber. Garnish with coriander, if liked.

**Serves 4 as a starter**
Preparation time: 30 minutes, plus making chilli sauce
Cooking time: 10 minutes

# Leek and Filo Parcels

*These filo parcels make an elegant dinner party starter.*

40 g/1½ oz butter
500 g/1 lb leeks, trimmed cleaned and
   thinly sliced
1 garlic clove, crushed
4 tablespoons crème fraîche or fromage
   frais
1 tablespoon chopped fresh chervil
freshly grated nutmeg
25 g/1 oz fresh white breadcrumbs
25 g/1 oz freshly grated vegetarian
   Parmesan cheese
8 large sheets filo pastry, thawed if
   frozen
extra virgin olive oil, to brush
salt and pepper
extra crème fraîche, to serve
chervil sprigs, to garnish

**1** Melt half the butter in a frying pan, add the leeks and garlic and fry gently for 4-5 minutes until the leeks are tender. Remove from the heat, cool slightly and stir in the crème fraîche or fromage frais, chervil, nutmeg, salt and pepper.
**2** Melt the remaining butter in another pan, add the breadcrumbs and stir-fry for 4-5 minutes until golden. Stir into the leek mixture with the Parmesan.
**3** Cut each sheet of pastry length-ways into 3 strips. Brush one strip with oil, place a second on top and brush again (keep the remaining sheets covered with a damp tea towel as you work, to prevent the pastry from drying out).
**4** Place a heaped tablespoonful of the leek mixture at one end of the pastry. Fold over on the diagonal and continue folding along the length of the pastry to enclose the filling. Brush with oil and transfer to an oiled baking sheet. Repeat to make 12 triangles.
**5** Bake in a preheated oven, 200°C (400°F), Gas Mark 6, for 20-25 minutes until golden. Serve with extra crème fraîche, garnish with chervil.

**Serves 4-6**
Preparation time: 15 minutes
Cooking time: 30-35 minutes
Oven temperature: 200°C (400°F),
Gas Mark 6

## Bruschetta

**4 thick slices day old rustic-style bread**
**2 garlic cloves**
**extra virgin olive oil, to drizzle**

**1** Toast the bread lightly on both sides, either over a barbecue or under a hot grill. Immediately rub the toast all over with the garlic cloves and drizzle with as much olive oil as liked. Either serve at once or top with any of the suggested toppings.

**Serves 4**
Preparation time: 2 minutes
Cooking time: 3-4 minutes

**All topping recipes serve 4**

## Grilled Tomato and Olive Paste Topping

**4 firm ripe plum tomatoes, quartered**
**extra virgin olive oil**
**1 quantity Bruschetta (see page left)**
**2 tablespoons Olive Paste (see page 9)**
**a few shredded basil leaves**
**salt and pepper**

**1** Place the plum tomatoes in a roasting pan with a little oil and place under a hot grill for 10 minutes until the plum tomatoes are tender and golden.
**2** Prepare the bruschetta. Prepare the olive paste according to the recipe on page 9.
**3** Spread the olive paste over one side of each bruschetta and top with the grilled tomatoes, basil leaves and salt and pepper. Serve at once.

Preparation time: 5 minutes, plus making bruschetta and olive paste
Cooking time: 14 minutes

## Aubergine and Cumin Topping

1 tablespoon cumin seeds
75 ml/3 fl oz extra virgin olive oil
1 teaspoon grated lemon rind
2 small aubergines, sliced
1 quantity Bruschetta (see left)
125 g/4 oz rocket leaves
1 tablespoon French Dressing (see
    page 91)

**1** Dry-fry the cumin seeds in a small frying pan until they start to pop and give off a smoky aroma. Carefully add the oil and lemon rind, remove from the heat and leave to infuse for several hours. Strain the oil into a bowl and reserve.
**2** Trim the aubergines and cut each one lengthways into 4 thick slices. Brush lightly with the cumin-scented oil and place under a preheated grill. Cook for 6-8 minutes until charred, turn over and repeat. Allow to cool to room temperature.
**3** Just before serving, prepare the bruschetta. Top with the aubergine slices and drizzle over a little of the cumin oil.
**4** Toss the rocket leaves with the French dressing, arrange over the aubergines and drizzle over the remaining cumin oil. Serve at once.

Preparation time: 5 minutes, plus infusing time and making bruschetta and dressing
Cooking time: 18-20 minutes

## Wild and Cultivated Mushroom Topping

15 g/½ oz dried ceps
100 ml/3½ fl oz boiling water
2 tablespoons extra virgin olive oil, plus
    extra to drizzle
1 garlic clove, crushed
375 g/12 oz mixed cultivated
    mushrooms, sliced
1 tablespoon chopped fresh thyme
1 quantity Bruschetta (see left)
1 tablespoon chopped fresh parsley
freshly grated vegetarian Parmesan
    cheese, to serve
salt and pepper

**1** Soak the ceps in the boiling water for 20 minutes, then drain, reserving the liquid. Slice the ceps.
**2** Heat the oil in a frying pan, add the garlic, ceps, sliced mushrooms and thyme and stir-fry for 3-4 minutes until golden. Add the reserved cep liquid, cover and cook over a low heat for 5 minutes.
**3** Meanwhile prepare the bruschetta. Spoon on the mushroom mixture, top with the parsley and Parmesan and season well.

Preparation time: 10 minutes, plus 20 minutes soaking and making bruschetta
Cooking time: 10 minutes

## Escarole and Grilled Pepper Topping

1 red pepper, cored, deseeded and
    quartered
1 yellow pepper, cored, deseeded and
    quartered
2 tablespoons hazelnut oil
2 garlic cloves, sliced
1 tablespoon grated lemon rind
25 g/1 oz sultanas
25 g/1 oz flaked hazelnuts
175 g/6 oz escarole, shredded
1 quantity Bruschetta (see left)
salt and pepper

**1** Grill the pepper quarters for 6-8 minutes on each until charred and tender. Transfer to a plastic bag and set aside until cool enough to handle. Peel off the skin from the peppers and slice the flesh.
**2** Heat the oil in a frying pan, add the garlic, lemon rind, sultanas and hazelnuts and fry gently for 5 minutes until golden. Add the escarole and cook over a low heat for 5 minutes until tender.
**3** Meanwhile, prepare the bruschetta.
**4** Divide the escarole mixture between the bruschetta and top with the grilled peppers. Serve at once.

Preparation time: 15 minutes, plus making bruschetta
Cooking time: 18-20 minutes

## *Baked Pasta with Aubergine and Pepper*

4 tablespoons extra virgin olive oil
1 large aubergine, diced
1 onion, chopped
2 red peppers, cored, deseeded and diced
1 tablespoon dried oregano
175 g/6 oz dried penne
1 quantity Fresh Tomato Sauce (see page 126)
2 egg yolks
250 g/8 oz crème fraîche or fromage frais
2 tablespoons milk
125 g/4 oz vegetarian feta cheese, diced
salt and pepper

**1** First make the tomato sauce according to the recipe on page 126.
**2** Meanwhile, heat half the oil in a large frying pan, add the aubergine and stir-fry over a medium heat for 6-8 minutes until golden and tender. Remove with a slotted spoon. Add the remaining oil and fry the onion, peppers and oregano for 10 minutes.
**3** Cook the pasta according to the packet instructions. Drain well and immediately toss with the tomato sauce and vegetables, seasoning to taste. Spoon into a deep, oiled, 20 x 30 cm/8 x 12 inch baking dish.
**4** Beat together the remaining ingredients until evenly combined and carefully pour over the pasta mixture to cover. Transfer to a preheated oven, 180°C (350°F), Gas Mark 4, and bake for 35-40 minutes until the topping is set and golden. Leave to sit for 5 minutes and then cut into squares. Serve with a mixed salad.

**Serves 4-6**
Preparation time: 15 minutes, plus making sauce
Cooking time: 50 minutes
Oven temperature: 180°C (350°F), Gas Mark 4

## Fresh Pasta

*Making fresh pasta is far more practical with the aid of a pasta machine which although expensive is well worth it. The first time you make the sheets, take them to the second thinnest setting on the machine and then progress to the thinnest when you feel confident. I use special pasta flour, which is far finer than plain flour. Some supermarkets sell this flour, or try an Italian delicatessen.*

**250 g/8 oz pasta flour, plus extra for dusting**
**3 teaspoons salt**
**2 eggs, plus 1 egg yolk**
**1 tablespoon extra virgin olive oil**
**1-2 tablespoons cold water**
**1 quantity Pesto Sauce (see page 126) or ½ quantity Fresh Tomato Sauce (see page 126)**

**1** Sift the flour and 1 teaspoon salt into a bowl, make a well in the centre and gradually work in the eggs, egg yolk, oil and enough water to form a soft dough.
**2** Turn out on to a lightly floured surface and knead gently for 5 minutes until the dough is smooth and elastic. Brush with a little oil, cover and leave to rest for 30 minutes.
**3** Divide the dough into 8 pieces. Take one piece and pat into a flattish rectangle. With the pasta rolling machine set at its widest

setting, feed the dough through twice. Repeat the process at each setting, feeding the sheet of dough through the rollers lengthways, until the sheet is long and very thin. Cut the sheet in half widthways and hang over a pole to dry for 5 minutes.
**4** Repeat with the remaining pieces of dough to make 16 sheets of pasta. Pass each sheet through either the tagliatelle or linguine cutter of the machine, hanging the noodles over the pole to dry for a further 5 minutes. Taking about 12 noodles at a time, wind them into 'nests' and place on a floured tea towel.

**5** Bring a large saucepan of water (at least 3.5 litres/6 pints) to a rolling boil. Add 2 teaspoons of salt and as soon as the water boils again drop in the pasta 'nests'. Return to the boil and cook for 2-3 minutes until the pasta is *al dente*.
**6** Drain the pasta, return to the pan, toss in a sauce of your choice and serve at once.

**Serves 4 as a main course or 6 as a starter**
Preparation time: 20 minutes, plus 40 minutes resting time
Cooking time: 2-3 minutes

## Spaghetti with Tomato and Egg Sauce

½ quantity Quick Tomato Sauce (see page 126)

2 eggs

25 g/1 oz freshly grated vegetarian Parmesan cheese

4 tablespoons mascarpone cheese or single cream

500 g/1 lb fresh spaghetti

25 g/1 oz butter

salt and pepper

**1** Make the quick tomato sauce according to the recipe on page 126 and keep warm.

**2** Beat together the eggs, Parmesan, mascarpone or cream and salt and pepper until evenly combined.

**3** Bring a large saucepan of water to a rolling boil, add the salt and the pasta, return to the boil and cook over a medium heat for 3-4 minutes until the pasta is *al dente*. Drain well, toss with the butter and plenty of pepper and transfer to a large, warm serving bowl.

**4** Remove the tomato sauce from the heat and whisk in the egg mixture.

Pour over the spaghetti, toss well and serve at once.

**Serves 4**
Preparation time: 5 minutes, plus making tomato sauce
Cooking time: 5 minutes, plus sauce

# Ian's Favourite Pasta Supper

*This dish is dedicated to my husband, who has made this quick and simple supper dish his own.*

1 teaspoon salt
350 g/12 oz dried pasta shapes
6 tablespoons extra virgin olive oil
2 garlic cloves, sliced
1 teaspoon grated lemon rind
1 dried red chilli, deseeded and crushed

500 g/1 lb courgettes, sliced thinly
1 tablespoon shredded basil leaves
2-3 tablespoons Red Pesto
(see page 126)
pepper

**1** Bring a large saucepan of water to a rolling boil, add the salt and the pasta shapes, return to the boil and cook over a medium heat for 10-12 minutes until the pasta is *al dente*.
**2** Meanwhile, heat 2 tablespoons of the oil in a deep frying pan, add the garlic, lemon rind and chilli and fry for 2-3 minutes until just golden. Add the courgettes and basil and stir-fry for a further 3-4 minutes, until golden.
**3** Drain the pasta and stir into the courgette pan with the remaining oil, red pesto and plenty of freshly ground black pepper. Toss well over a low heat for 1 minute and serve immediately.

**Serves 4**
Preparation time: 10 minutes
Cooking time: 12-15 minutes

VARIATION

# Pasta with Lettuce and Peas

1 teaspoon salt
350 g/12 oz dried pasta
6 tablespoons hazelnut or extra virgin olive oil
1 leek, trimmed, cleaned and thinly sliced
2 garlic cloves, chopped
2 teaspoons grated lime rind
2 little gem lettuces, shredded roughly
250 g/8 oz frozen peas, thawed
4 tablespoons chopped fresh chives
2 tablespoons lime juice
4 tablespoons soured cream
salt and pepper

**1** Bring a large saucepan of water to a rolling boil, add the salt and the dried pasta, return to the boil and cook over a medium heat for 10-12 minutes until *al dente*.
**2** Meanwhile, heat half the oil in a pan, add the leek, garlic and lime rind and fry gently for 3 minutes. Add the lettuce, peas, chives and lime juice, cover and cook over a low heat for about 4-5 minutes until the lettuce and peas are cooked.
**3** Drain the cooked pasta, toss with the remaining oil, soured cream, and pepper and stir into the lettuce mixture. Serve at once.

**Serves 4**
Preparation time: 10 minutes
Cooking time: 12-15 minutes

# Beetroot Ravioli with Dill Cream

**1 quantity Fresh Pasta (see page 30)**
FILLING:
**1 tablespoon extra virgin olive oil**
**1 small onion, chopped finely**
**½ teaspoon caraway seeds**
**175 g/6 oz cooked beetroot**
**175 g/6 oz ricotta or curd cheese**
**25 g/1 oz homemade dried breadcrumbs**
**1 egg yolk**
**2 tablespoons freshly grated vegetarian Parmesan cheese**
**grated nutmeg**
DILL CREAM:
**4 tablespoons walnut oil**
**4 tablespoons chopped fresh dill**
**1 tablespoon drained green peppercorns in brine, crushed**
**6 tablespoons crème fraîche or fromage frais**
**salt and pepper**

**1** Make the pasta dough, according to the recipe on page 30. Wrap in clingfilm and leave to rest until the dough is required.
**2** For the filling. Heat the oil in a frying pan, add the onion and caraway seeds and fry over a medium heat for 5 minutes until light golden. Add the beetroot and cook for a further 5 minutes.
**3** Process the beetroot mixture in a blender until smooth, allow to cool. Beat in the ricotta or curd cheese, breadcrumbs, egg yolk, Parmesan and nutmeg, season to taste.
**4** Roll out the dough to form 8 pasta sheets (see page 30), cut each in half widthways. Lay one sheet on a floured surface and place 5 heaped teaspoons of the filling at 2.5 cm/ 1 inch intervals over the dough (see page 9).
**5** Dampen around the mounds with a wet pastry brush and lay a second sheet of pasta over the top, press down around the mounds to seal well. Cut into ravioli rounds with a stamp or into squares using a sharp knife and place on a floured tea towel. Repeat to make 40 ravioli.
**6** Bring a large pan of water to a rolling boil and add 2 teaspoons of salt. Meanwhile, make the sauce. Heat the oil in a small pan, add the chopped dill and green peppercorns and remove from the heat. Stir in the crème fraîche.
**7** Drop the ravioli into the boiling water, return to the boil and cook for 3-4 minutes until al dente. Drain well, transfer to a warm serving dish and toss with the dill cream and black pepper. Serve at once.

**Serves 4-6**
Preparation time: 1 hour, including making pasta
Cooking time: 22-25 minutes

# Baked Tortellini with Savoy Cabbage

*Fresh tortellini is widely available in supermarkets and comes with a variety of tasty fillings. I use spinach and ricotta stuffed pasta, but choose which ever is your favourite filling.*

½ **savoy cabbage (250 g/8 oz shredded weight)**
2 **tablespoons extra virgin olive oil, plus extra for oiling**
2 **small onions, sliced thinly**
2 **garlic cloves, crushed**
75 **g/3 oz drained sun-dried tomatoes in oil, sliced**
1 **tablespoon chopped fresh tarragon**
375 **g/12 oz fresh tortellini**
1 **quantity Classic White Sauce (see page 127)**
65 **g/2½ oz vegetarian Cheshire cheese, grated**
**salt and pepper**

**1** Finely shred the savoy cabbage, discarding the thick central core. Blanch in a large pan of lightly salted, boiling water for 1 minute. Drain, refresh under cold water and dry well on paper towels.
**2** Heat the oil in a large frying pan, add the onion and garlic and cook for 5 minutes. Stir in the blanched cabbage, sun-dried tomatoes and tarragon and set aside.

**3** Cook the tortellini according to the packet instructions, drain, refresh under cold running water and pat dry on paper towels.
**4** Toss all of the cooked pasta with the cabbage and onion mixture and spoon into an oiled baking dish. Add 50 g/2 oz of the grated cheese to the white sauce and pour over the cabbage and onion mixture. Scatter the top with grated cheese. Bake in a preheated oven, 200°C

(400°F), Gas Mark 6, for 30-35 minutes until bubbling and golden.
**Serves 6-8**
Preparation time: 20 minutes, plus making white sauce
Cooking time: 35-40 minutes, plus sauce
Oven temperature: 200°C (400°F), Gas Mark 6

# Spinach and Ricotta Gnocchi

*These delicate gnocchi are piped straight into a pan of boiling water,*
*making them quicker and easier to prepare than potato gnocchi.*

125 g/4 oz frozen leaf spinach,
   thawed
250 g/8 oz ricotta cheese
2 small eggs (size 5), beaten
50 g/2 oz freshly grated vegetarian
   Parmesan cheese
1 tablespoon chopped fresh basil
50 g/2 oz plain flour
salt and pepper

SAUCE:
50 g/2 oz unsalted butter
1 garlic clove, crushed
1 red chilli, deseeded and chopped
50-65 g/2-2½ oz freshly grated
   vegetarian Parmesan cheese

**1** Squeeze out the excess water from the spinach until dry and chop finely.
Place in a blender with the ricotta and process until smooth. Beat in the eggs,
cheese and basil and enough flour to form a soft, slightly tacky dough.
**2** Bring a large pan of salted water to the boil. Transfer the spinach mixture to
a piping bag fitted with a large plain nozzle. As soon as the water is boiling
pipe about 12 short lengths of gnocchi into the water, using a sharp knife to
cut away from the nozzle as you pipe.
**3** Cook the gnocchi for 2-3 minutes until they rise to the surface, then remove
with a slotted spoon, drain on paper towels and transfer to a warmed serving
dish. Keep warm while cooking the remaining gnocchi.
**4** Melt the butter in a small pan and fry the garlic and chilli for 2 minutes.
Pour over the gnocchi and toss well. Sprinkle with the cheese and serve
at once.

**Serves 4-6**
Preparation time: 20 minutes
Cooking time: 12-15 minutes

**VARIATION**
Cook the gnocchi as above and toss with ½ quantity of the Fresh Tomato Sauce
(see page 126).

# Thai Noodles with Vegetables and Tofu

*A classic noodle dish, similar to many found on Thai menus.*

250 g/8 oz tofu (bean curd), cubed
2 tablespoons dark soy sauce
1 teaspoon grated lime rind
1.75 litres/3 pints Vegetable Stock (see page 126)
2 slices fresh root ginger
2 garlic cloves
2 coriander sprigs
2 stalks lemon grass, crushed
1 red chilli, bruised
175 g/6 oz dried egg noodles
125 g/4 oz shiitake or button mushrooms, sliced
2 large carrots, cut into matchsticks
125 g/4 oz snap peas
125 g/4 oz Chinese cabbage, shredded
2 tablespoons chopped fresh coriander
salt and pepper

**1** Put the tofu in a shallow dish with the soy sauce and lime rind and leave to marinate for 30 minutes.
**2** Meanwhile, put the vegetable stock into a large saucepan and add the ginger, garlic, coriander, lemon grass and chilli. Bring the mixture to the boil, cover and simmer gently for 30 minutes.
**3** Strain the stock into a pan, return to the boil and plunge in the noodles. Add the marinated tofu together with its marinade, and mushrooms. Simmer gently for 4 minutes.
**4** Stir in the carrots, snap peas, Chinese cabbage and coriander and cook for a further 3-4 minutes until all the vegetables are tender. Taste and adjust the seasoning and serve immediately.

**Serves 4**
Preparation time: 20 minutes
Cooking time: 40 minutes

# Egg-fried Noodles with Vegetables and Tofu

*Many Chinese and Asian dishes require a fair amount of preparation, but this can often be done well in advance; the cooking times are always so short that the lengthy preparation is soon forgotten.*

vegetable oil, for deep frying
250 g/8 oz plain tofu (bean curd), cubed
75 g/3 oz dried thread egg noodles
125 g/4 oz broccoli florets
125 g/4 oz baby sweetcorn, halved
3 tablespoons light soy sauce
1 tablespoon lemon juice
1 teaspoon sugar
1 teaspoon chilli sauce
3 tablespoons sunflower oil
1 garlic clove, chopped
1 red chilli, deseeded and sliced
2 eggs, lightly beaten
125 g/4 oz drained water chestnuts, sliced

**1** Heat about 5 cm/2 inches of vegetable oil in a heavy-bottomed saucepan until a cube of bread browns in 30 seconds. Add the tofu and fry for 3-4 minutes until crisp and lightly golden. Drain the tofu on paper towels.
**2** Cook the noodles according to the packet instructions, drain, refresh under cold water and dry well on paper towels.
**3** Blanch the broccoli and sweetcorn in a saucepan of boiling water for 1 minute, drain, refresh under cold water and pat dry with paper towels. Mix together the soy sauce, lemon juice, sugar and chilli sauce.
**4** Heat the sunflower oil in a wok or large frying pan, add the garlic and chilli and stir-fry for 3 minutes. Add the noodles and stir-fry for 5 minutes, until golden and starting to crisp up.
**5** Stir in the eggs, and stir-fry for 1 minute, then stir in the sauce, tofu, vegetables and water chestnuts and stir-fry for a further 2-3 minutes until heated through. Serve at once.

**Serves 4**
Preparation time: 20 minutes
Cooking time: 15-18 minutes

## *Brown Rice and Vegetable Pilaf*

2 tablespoons extra virgin olive oil
1 onion, chopped
2 garlic cloves, chopped
1 teaspoon roasted coriander seeds, crushed
1 teaspoon roasted cumin seeds, crushed
2 dried red chillies, crushed
1 teaspoon ground cinnamon
2 large carrots, sliced
2 celery sticks, sliced
375 g/12 oz brown rice
900 ml/1½ pints Vegetable Stock (see page 126)
125 g/4 oz French beans, halved
50 g/2 oz green peas, thawed if frozen
50 g/2 oz dried figs, chopped
50 g/2 oz cashew nuts, toasted
2 tablespoons chopped fresh coriander or parsley
salt and pepper

**1** Heat the olive oil in a large saucepan, add the onion, garlic and spices and fry gently for 5 minutes. Add the sliced carrots and celery and fry for a further 5 minutes, season to taste.

**2** Add the rice, stir-fry for 1 minute and then pour in the stock. Bring to the boil, cover and simmer over a gentle heat for 20 minutes. Add all the remaining ingredients and cook for a further 10 -15 minutes until the rice is cooked and the vegetables are tender.

**Serves 4-6**
Preparation time: 25 minutes
Cooking time: 50 minutes

## Tuscan Stew with Polenta Topping

*A rich stew topped with triangles of polenta. Quick-cook polenta is readily available.*

1 litre/1¾ pints water
1 teaspoon salt
175 g/6 oz quick-cook polenta
25 g/1 oz butter
50 g/2 oz vegetarian Cheddar cheese, grated
25g/1 oz Parmesan cheese, grated

FILLING:

4 tablespoons extra virgin olive oil, plus extra for greasing and brushing
1 medium aubergine, diced
2 garlic cloves, crushed
1 red onion, sliced
1 tablespoon chopped fresh thyme
1 red pepper, deseeded and sliced
2 courgettes, diced
2 celery sticks, sliced
1 x 400 g/14 oz can chopped tomatoes
1 x 400 g/14 oz can flageolet beans, plus their liquid
2 tablespoons chopped fresh basil
salt and pepper

**1** Put the water and salt into a large saucepan and bring to the boil. Whisk in the polenta and simmer, stirring occasionally, for 5-6 minutes until the polenta is thickened and leaves the sides of the pan. Stir in the butter and Cheddar cheese. Spoon into a greased 23 x 33 cm/9 x 13 inch Swiss roll tin. Smooth the surface and leave to set (takes about 20 minutes).
**2** Meanwhile, make the filling. Heat half the oil in a large saucepan and fry the aubergines for 6-8 minutes until golden and tender. Remove with a slotted spoon and set aside. Add the remaining oil and the garlic, onion, thyme, pepper, courgettes, and celery and fry for 5 minutes.
**3** Add all the remaining ingredients, return the aubergines to the pan, bring to the boil and simmer over a gentle heat for 45 minutes. Season to taste and keep warm.
**4** Turn out the polenta. Cut into 12 squares, then into triangles. Then cut each triangle in half vertically to make 48 polenta triangles.
**5** Spoon the filling into a 20 x 25 cm/8 x 10 inch baking dish, and arrange the polenta triangles, overlapping, on top. Brush with oil, sprinkle over the Parmesan and place under a hot grill for 10-12 minutes until bubbling and golden.

### Serves 6-8
Preparation time: 40 minutes, plus setting time
Cooking time: 1¼ hours

# Tabbouleh with Raisins, Pistachios and Cracked Pepper

*Tabbouleh is a Middle Eastern and North African salad dish made with bulgar wheat. Although the grains are soaked before a dressing is added they do not loose their nutty texture.*

250 g/8 oz bulgar wheat
1 small red onion, chopped finely
2 tablespoons chopped fresh
   coriander
2 tab'-- ~~pped fresh mint
75 g/3 oz .
120 ml/4 fl oz extra virgin olive oil
50 ml/2 fl oz lemon juice
1 tablespoon cracked black pepper
2 teaspoons ground coriander
1 teaspoon ground cinnamon
50 g/2 oz pistachio nuts, chopped
50 g/2 oz stoned black olives,
   chopped
salt

**1** Place the bulgar wheat in a bowl and add plenty of cold water. Set aside to soak for 30 minutes then drain off any remaining water.
**2** Mix the bulgar wheat with the onion, herbs, raisins, olive oil, lemon juice, pepper and spices, stirring well until evenly blended. Chill for 1 hour for the flavours to develop.

**3** Remove the salad from the refrigerator and return to room temperature. Stir in the nuts and olives, season to taste and serve at once.

**Serves 4**
Preparation time: 10 minutes, plus 1 hour chilling time

# Pumpkin and Sage Risotto with Pine Nut Sauce

*This is a rich and creamy risotto, with the slightly unusual inclusion of a pine nut sauce. It has become one of my standard dinner party dishes and is always met with an appreciative silence. When pumpkin is not available use 500 g/1 lb butternut squash instead and substitute rosemary for the sage.*

2 tablespoons extra virgin olive oil
1 large onion, finely chopped
1 garlic clove, chopped
1-2 tablespoons chopped fresh sage
375 g/12 oz arborio rice
500 g/1 lb pumpkin flesh, diced
1 litre/1¾ pints boiling Vegetable
　Stock (see page 126)

25 g/1 oz pine nuts, toasted
25 g/1 oz freshly grated vegetarian
　Parmesan cheese
4 tablespoons milk
pinch of freshly grated nutmeg
salt and pepper

**1** Heat the oil in a large saucepan and fry the onion, garlic and sage for about 5 minutes until golden. Add the rice and pumpkin and stir-fry for 1 minute until all the rice grains are well coated in oil.
**2** Add 150 ml/¼ pint of stock and simmer, stirring until absorbed. Continue to add the stock a little at a time, stirring frequently, for about 25 minutes, until the rice is creamy and all the liquid is absorbed.
**3** Meanwhile, process the pine nuts, cheese, milk and nutmeg in a blender until smooth. Stir into the risotto, with the final addition of stock, and simmer for a further 5 minutes. Season to taste and serve at once.

**Serves 4**
Preparation time: 20 minutes
Cooking time: 35-40 minutes

VARIATION

# Onion Risotto

25 g/1 oz butter
2 tablespoons extra virgin olive oil
500 g/1 lb baby onions
2 tablespoons chopped fresh thyme
375 g/12 oz easy-cook brown risotto
　rice
150 ml/¼ pint light red wine
900 ml/1½ pints Vegetable Stock (see
　page 126)
125 g/4 oz drained sun-dried
　tomatoes in oil, chopped
1 tablespoon balsamic vinegar
4 tablespoons crème fraîche or
　fromage frais
salt and pepper
freshly grated vegetarian Parmesan
　cheese, to serve (optional)

**1** Melt the butter with the oil in a large frying pan, add the onions and cook over a low heat for 25 minutes until golden and caramelized, stirring occasionally.
**2** Add the thyme and rice and stir-fry for 1 minute, then pour in the red wine. Boil rapidly for 5 minutes until reduced. Gradually add the stock, and simmer gently, stirring frequently until all the stock is absorbed.
**3** Stir in all the remaining ingredients, season to taste and serve at once with Parmesan, if liked.

**Serves 4**
Preparation time: 40 minutes
Cooking time: 55-60 minutes

## Bulgar Patties Stuffed with Spiced Cheese

75 g/3 oz bulgar wheat, rinsed
250 ml/8 fl oz boiling Vegetable Stock
  (see page 126)
250 g/8 oz potatoes, cubed
1 tablespoon sunflower oil
½ red onion, chopped very finely
1 garlic clove, crushed

15 g/½ oz cashew nuts, chopped
15 g/½ oz raisins, chopped
1 tablespoon chopped fresh coriander
1 egg yolk
25 g/1 oz plain flour
vegetable oil, for shallow frying
yogurt and lemon wedges, to serve
salt and pepper
FILLING:
50 g/2 oz mozzarella cheese, diced
¼ teaspoon chilli powder
¼ teaspoon ground cinnamon
½ teaspoon grated lemon rind

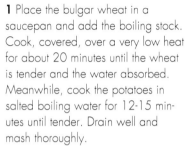

**1** Place the bulgar wheat in a saucepan and add the boiling stock. Cook, covered, over a very low heat for about 20 minutes until the wheat is tender and the water absorbed. Meanwhile, cook the potatoes in salted boiling water for 12-15 minutes until tender. Drain well and mash thoroughly.

**2** Heat the oil in a frying pan and fry the onion, garlic, nuts, raisins and coriander for 5 minutes. Combine with the wheat, potatoes, egg yolk and flour in a blender and process until fairly smooth. Season to taste and leave the mixture to go cold.

**3** In a small bowl mix together the filling ingredients. Divide the bulgar mixture into 12 balls. Press a hollow into the middle of each one and stuff with some of the cheese mixture. Press the bulgar mixture back into a ball shape, totally enclosing the filling, and form into patties.

**4** Heat 1 cm/½ inch oil in a non-stick frying pan and cook the patties in batches over a low heat for 3-4 minutes on each side until golden. Drain on paper towels and serve hot with yogurt and wedges of lemon.

**Serves 4**
Preparation time: 40 minutes
Cooking time: 35-40 minutes

## Spring Herb Risotto With Sprouting Broccoli and Goats' Cheese

*A slightly unusual risotto where goats' cheese is added just before serving instead of the more usual Parmesan cheese. The herbs are blanched in boiling water, which mellows their flavour.*

300 ml/½ pint water
4 large handfuls mixed spring herbs
    (such as basil, chervil, chives and
    parsley)
125 g/4 oz soft goats' cheese
250 g/8 oz sprouting broccoli
5 tablespoons extra virgin olive oil
1 small onion, chopped finely
2 garlic cloves, crushed
375 g/12 oz arborio rice
150 ml/¼ pint dry white wine
750 ml/1¼ pints Vegetable Stock
    (see page 126)
salt and pepper

**1** Put the water in a saucepan, bring to the boil and add the herbs. Return to the boil, then strain, reserving the liquid, and immediately rinse the herbs under cold water. Drain and dry on paper towels.
**2** Put all of the herbs, and the goats' cheese in a blender and process until smooth, then set aside.

**3** Bring the reserved herb liquid to the boil, add the sprouting broccoli and cook for 2 minutes. Strain, reserving the liquid, and rinse the broccoli under cold water. Pat dry on paper towels.
**4** Heat 4 tablespoons of the oil in a large saucepan, add the onion and garlic and fry gently for 5 minutes. Add the rice and stir-fry for 1 minute until all the grains are coated with the oil. Pour in the wine and boil rapidly for 10 minutes until all the liquid is absorbed.
**5** Add the vegetable stock and

reserved herb liquid a little at a time, and simmer, stirring frequently, until all of the liquid is absorbed, about 25 minutes.
**6** Heat the remaining oil in a small frying pan, add the broccoli and fry gently for 3 minutes. Stir the herbed cheese mixture into the risotto with the seasonings, heat through and serve at once topped with the cooked broccoli.

**Serves 4**
Preparation time: 20 minutes
Cooking time: 50-55 minutes

# Vegetable Biryani

*A biryani is an Indian rice dish made with either meat or vegetables, or a combination of both. It is dry, as there is no sauce as such, and so it is usual to serve a biryani with other curry dishes, and dhal in particular.*

250 g/8 oz basmati rice, rinsed
6 tablespoons sunflower oil
2 large onions, sliced thinly
2 garlic cloves, crushed
2 teaspoons grated root ginger
250 g/8 oz sweet potato, diced
2 large carrots, diced
1 tablespoon curry paste
2 teaspoons ground turmeric
1 teaspoon ground cinnamon
1 teaspoon chilli powder

300 ml/½ pint Vegetable Stock (see page 126)
4 ripe tomatoes, skinned, deseeded and diced
175 g/6 oz cauliflower florets
125 g/4 oz frozen peas, thawed
50 g/2 oz cashew nuts, toasted
2 tablespoons chopped fresh coriander
salt and pepper
2 hard-boiled eggs, quartered, to serve

**1** Bring a large saucepan of salted water to a rolling boil, add the basmati rice and return to a simmer. Cook gently for 5 minutes. Drain, refresh under cold water and drain again. Spread the rice out on a large baking sheet and set aside to dry.

**2** Heat 2 tablespoons of oil in a frying pan, add half the onion and fry over a medium heat for 10 minutes until very crisp and golden. Remove and drain on paper towels. Reserve for garnishing.

**3** Add the remaining oil to the pan and fry the remaining onion with the garlic and ginger for 5 minutes. Add the potato, carrot and spices and continue to fry for a further 10 minutes until light golden.

**4** Add the vegetable stock and tomatoes, bring to the boil, cover and simmer gently for 20 minutes. Add the cauliflower and peas and cook for a further 8-10 minutes until all the vegetables are tender.

**5** Stir in the rice, cashew nuts and coriander. Cook, stirring, for 3 minutes, then cover and remove from the heat. Leave to sit for 5 minutes before serving. Garnish with the crispy onions and egg quarters.

**Serves 4**
Preparation time: 25 minutes
Cooking time: 50-55 minutes, plus 5 minutes resting

---

VARIATION

# Gingered Rice with Carrots and Tomatoes

250 g/8 oz basmati rice, rinsed
4 tablespoons extra virgin olive oil
2 garlic cloves, crushed
1 tablespoon grated root ginger
4 carrots, sliced thinly
4 ripe tomatoes, skinned, deseeded and diced
2 cinnamon sticks, bruised
seeds from 3 cardamom pods, bruised
1 dried red chilli
1 tablespoon lemon juice
50 g/2 oz flaked almonds, toasted
salt and pepper

**1** Cook the rice in plenty of boiling, salted water for 5 minutes. Drain well, refresh under cold water and drain again. Spread out on a baking sheet and set aside to dry.

**2** Heat the oil in a wok or large frying pan, add the garlic, ginger and carrots and fry for 10 minutes. Add the tomatoes and spices and cook for a further 5 minutes.

**3** Stir in the rice, lemon juice, nuts and salt and pepper and stir-fry for 3-4 minutes until the rice is heated through. Serve at once.

**Serves 4**
Preparation time: 20 minutes
Cooking time: 20 minutes

## *Black Bean Chilli*

250 g/8 oz dried black kidney beans, soaked overnight
1.5 litres/2½ pints water
4 tablespoons extra virgin olive oil
250 g/8 oz small mushrooms, halved
1 large onion, chopped
2 garlic cloves, crushed
2 large potatoes, cubed
1 red or green pepper, cored, deseeded and diced
2 teaspoons ground coriander
1 teaspoon ground cumin
2 teaspoons hot chilli powder
450 ml/¾ pint passata (sieved tomatoes)
1 tablespoon lime juice
25 g/1 oz dark chocolate, chopped
2 tablespoons chopped fresh coriander
Avocado Salsa, to serve (see page 10) (optional)

**1** Drain the beans, place in a pan with the water. Bring to the boil, boil rapidly for 10 minutes. Reduce the heat, cover and simmer for 45 minutes.
**2** Heat half the oil in a pan and stir-fry the mushrooms for 5 minutes. Remove from the pan and reserve. Add the remaining oil to the pan with the onion, garlic, potato, pepper and spices, fry over a medium heat for 10 minutes.
**3** Drain the beans, reserving the liquid. Boil the liquid until reduced to 450 ml/¾ pint. Stir beans into the pan with the vegetables, add the stock, passata and mushrooms. Bring to the boil, cover and simmer for 30 minutes.
**4** Stir in the lime juice, chocolate and coriander and cook for a further 5 minutes. Serve piping hot topped with a spoonful of the avocado salsa, if using.

**Serves 8**
Preparation time: 20 minutes, plus soaking, plus making salsa (optional)
Cooking time: 1 hour 20 minutes

# Green Lentil and Vegetable Tagine with Couscous

*A tagine is the name of the clay dish in which stews are cooked in many North African countries such as Morocco and Tunisia. The classic accompaniment to a tagine stew is couscous - a type of ground pasta.*

125 g/4 oz green lentils, rinsed
600 ml/1 pint water
4 tablespoons extra virgin olive oil
2 small onions, cut into wedges
2 garlic cloves, chopped
1 tablespoon ground coriander
2 teaspoons ground cumin
1 teaspoon ground turmeric
1 teaspoon ground cinnamon
12 new potatoes, halved if large
2 large carrots, sliced thickly
250 g/8 oz couscous
2 courgettes, sliced
175 g/6 oz button mushrooms
300 ml/½ pint tomato juice
1 tablespoon tomato purée
2 tablespoons chilli sauce
125 g/4 oz ready-to-eat dried apricots, chopped
extra chilli sauce, to serve (optional)

**1** Put the lentils into a saucepan with the water. Bring to the boil, cover and simmer for 20 minutes.
**2** Meanwhile, heat half the oil in a large saucepan and fry the onion, garlic and spices for 5 minutes. Add the potatoes and carrots and fry for a further 5 minutes. Add the lentils with their cooking liquid, cover and simmer gently for 15 minutes.
**3** Rinse the couscous several times under cold running water to moisten all the grains and spread out on a large baking sheet. Sprinkle over a little water and then leave to soak for 15 minutes.
**4** Heat the remaining oil in a separate pan and fry the courgettes and mushrooms for 4-5 minutes until lightly golden. Add to the lentil mixture with the tomato juice, tomato purée, chilli sauce and dried apricots and return to the boil. Cook for a further 10 minutes until the vegetables and lentils are tender.
**5** Steam the couscous according to the instructions on the packet or over the stew in a double boiler, about 6-7 minutes. Transfer the couscous to a large warmed platter, spoon on the vegetable and lentil tagine and serve the juices separately with extra chilli sauce.

**Serves 4-6**
Preparation time: 40-45 minutes
Cooking time: 40 minutes

# Lentil, Aubergine and Coconut Dhal

*A delicious creamy, mildly spiced dhal which is a perfect accompaniment to the Vegetable Biryani (see page 48).*

175 g/6 oz split red lentils, rinsed
1 teaspoon ground turmeric
2 cinnamon sticks
750 ml/1¼ pints hot Vegetable Stock
    (see page 126)
4 tablespoons sunflower oil
4 red chillies, deseeded and chopped
2 garlic cloves, crushed
2 teaspoons fenugreek seeds
1 teaspoon yellow mustard seeds
1 large onion, chopped
1 aubergine, diced
2 teaspoons garam masala
2 tablespoons tomato purée
1 tablespoon lemon juice
50 g/2 oz creamed coconut
2 tablespoons chopped fresh coriander
salt and pepper
GARNISH:
natural yogurt,
chopped coriander
reserved spice mixture

**1** Place the lentils in a saucepan with the turmeric, cinnamon sticks and hot stock, bring to the boil, cover and simmer for 35-40 minutes until the lentils are softened and most of the stock is absorbed.
**2** Heat 1 tablespoon of the oil in a frying pan, add the chillies, garlic, fenugreek seeds and mustard seeds and fry for 5 minutes until golden. Remove from the pan and set aside. reserving a teaspoon for garnish.
**3** Add the remaining oil to the frying pan and fry the onion and aubergine for 10 minutes until golden. Return the chilli mixture to the pan with the garam masala, lentils, tomato purée and lemon juice. Simmer for 5 minutes, meanwhile mix together all the ingredients for the garnish.
**4** Stir in the creamed coconut until melted and the coriander, season to taste and serve at once topped with a spoonful of the garnish.

**Serves 4-6**
Preparation time: 25 minutes
Cooking time: 50 minutes

# Pumpkin, Chickpea and Banana Curry

*This combination of flavours may sound unusual, but they work very well together and are really tasty. Serve this curry with Gingered Rice with Carrots, Tomatoes and Almonds (see page 48).*

3 tablespoons sunflower oil
1 small onion, sliced
2 garlic cloves, chopped
2 teaspoons grated root ginger
1 teaspoon ground coriander
½ teaspoon ground cumin
½ teaspoon ground turmeric
¼ teaspoon ground cinnamon
500 g/1 lb pumpkin flesh, cubed

2 tablespoons hot curry paste
2 ripe tomatoes, chopped
2 dried red chillies
300 ml/½ pint Vegetable Stock (see page 126)
250 g/8 oz cooked chickpeas or 1 x 400 g/14 oz can chickpeas, drained
1 large under-ripe banana
1 tablespoon chopped fresh coriander

**1** Heat 2 tablespoons of the oil in a saucepan, add the onion, garlic, ginger and ground spices and fry over a medium heat for about 5-6 minutes until the onion is lightly browned.
**2** Place the pumpkin in a bowl, add the curry paste and toss well to evenly coat the pumpkin. Add the tomatoes, chillies and stock to the onion mixture, bring to the boil and simmer gently for 15 minutes.
**3** Meanwhile, heat the remaining oil in a non-stick frying pan, add the coated pumpkin and fry for 5 minutes until golden. Add to the tomato sauce with the chickpeas, cover and cook for 20 minutes until the pumpkin is tender.
**4** Peel the banana, slice thickly and stir into the curry 5 minutes before the end of the cooking time. Stir in the chopped coriander and serve hot with rice or naan bread.

**Serves 4**
Preparation time: 25 minutes
Cooking time: 50 minutes

VARIATION

# Chickpeas and Potatoes Baked in the Oven

4 tablespoons sunflower oil
1 onion, sliced
2 garlic cloves, chopped
1 tablespoon dried oregano
1 red chilli, deseeded and chopped finely
500 g/1 lb potatoes, cut into 1 cm/ ½ inch cubes
2 ripe tomatoes, chopped
2 thyme sprigs
2 rosemary sprigs
1 x 400 g/14 oz can chickpeas
½ vegetable stock cube
salt and pepper

**1** Heat the oil in a flameproof casserole and fry the onion, garlic, oregano and chilli for 5 minutes, add the potatoes and stir-fry for a further 10 minutes until golden.
**2** Add the tomatoes, herbs, chickpeas and their liquid and the stock cube. Cover the casserole and bake in a preheated oven, 190°C (375°F), Gas Mark 5, for 1 hour.

**Serves 4**
Preparation time: 20 minutes, plus overnight soaking
Cooking time: 2 hours
Oven temperature: 190°C (375°F), Gas Mark 5

# Chickpea Patties with Seasoned Yogurt

1 x 400 g/14 oz can chickpeas, drained
1 tablespoon tahini paste
25 g/1 oz cashew nuts, toasted and chopped
1 teaspoon ground coriander
½ teaspoon ground cumin
1 tablespoon lemon juice
1 teaspoon grated lemon rind
1 tablespoon chopped fresh coriander
2 tablespoons Greek yogurt
½ teaspoon baking powder
salt and pepper
vegetable oil, for oiling

SEASONED YOGURT:
1 tablespoon sunflower oil
1 teaspoon brown mustard seeds
¼ teaspoon freshly ground black pepper
1 teaspoon grated root ginger
175 g/6 oz Greek yogurt
2 tablespoons milk
1 tablespoon lime juice
a few coriander leaves, shredded

1 Place the chickpeas, tahini paste and cashew nuts in a blender and process to form a fairly smooth paste. Transfer to a bowl and beat in the remaining ingredients until evenly combined. Season to taste.
2 Using lightly oiled hands form the mixture into 16 balls, and flatten into patties. Transfer to a well-oiled baking sheet, bake in a preheated oven, 200°C (400°F), Gas Mark 6, for 20 minutes, turning once.
3 Meanwhile, make the yogurt sauce. Heat the oil in a small frying pan and fry the mustard seeds, pepper and ginger for 3-4 minutes until golden. Allow to cool slightly then stir into the yogurt with the milk, lime juice, coriander, and seasoning.
4 Serve the patties warm with the yogurt sauce or cool, chill for 1 hour and serve in pitta pockets with salad and a spoonful of yogurt sauce.

**Serves 4**
Preparation time: 15 minutes
Cooking time: 20 minutes
Oven temperature: 200°F (400°F), Gas Mark 6

# Speedy Mixed Baked Beans

*You may look at the cooking time and decide 'speedy' is a slight exaggeration, but the traditional method for Boston Baked Beans takes 6 hours to cook, plus overnight soaking of the beans.*

1 x 400 g/14 oz can red kidney beans
1 x 400 g/14 oz can haricot beans
1 x 400 g/14 oz can aduki beans
250 ml/8 fl oz pint passata (sieved tomatoes)
2 tablespoons molasses
½ tablespoon wholegrain mustard
1 tablespoon vegetarian Worcestershire sauce or dark soy sauce
½ teaspoon salt
pinch of ground cloves
1 large onion, chopped finely
2 carrots, diced
2 celery sticks, chopped
2 bay leaves
4 tablespoons chopped fresh parsley
grated vegetarian Cheddar cheese, to serve (optional)
pepper

**1** Strain the liquid from the beans and pour half into a bowl, discarding the rest. Whisk the passata, molasses, mustard, Worcestershire sauce or soy, salt and cloves into the liquid until evenly combined.
**2** Place the beans and all the remaining ingredients into a casserole and

stir in the liquid. Cover with a tight-fitting lid. Transfer to a preheated oven, 180°C (350°F), Gas Mark 4, and bake for 2 hours. Stir in the parsley and serve in warm bowls topped with the cheese, if using.

**Serves 6-8**
Preparation time: 15 minutes
Cooking time: 2 hours
Oven temperature: 180°C (350°F), Gas Mark 4

VARIATION

# Crusted Beans

Combine 50 g/2 oz fresh wholemeal breadcrumbs with 50 g/2 oz grated Cheddar and 25 g/1 oz ground almonds. Sprinkle over the beans after 1½ hours and return to the oven, uncovered, for a further 30 minutes to crisp up the topping.

# Cannellini Beans with Leeks and Rocket

*The contrast between the creaminess of the beans and their sauce is nicely balanced by the rocket, a peppery herb, stirred in at the last minute until it is just wilted.*

125 g/4 oz dried cannellini beans,
   soaked overnight
1.2 litres/2 pints water
2 tablespoons walnut oil
2 leeks, trimmed, cleaned and sliced
1 tablespoon mustard seeds

1 garlic clove, crushed
125 g/4 oz French beans, halved
75 ml/3 fl oz double cream
125 g/4 oz rocket
2 tablespoons chopped fresh chives
salt and pepper

**1** Drain the beans and place in a pan with the water. Bring to the boil and boil rapidly for 10 minutes. Reduce the heat and simmer gently for 45-50 minutes until the beans are tender.
**2** Strain the liquid from the beans into a pan and boil rapidly until reduced to 300 ml/½ pint. Reserve.
**3** Heat the oil in a saucepan and fry the leeks, mustard seeds and garlic for 5 minutes. Add the drained beans, French beans and reduced stock and simmer gently for 5 minutes until the French beans are tender. Stir in the cream and boil for 2-3 minutes until slightly reduced. Stir in the rocket and chives, cover and cook gently for 2-3 minutes until the rocket is wilted. Season to taste and serve at once.

**Serves 4-6**
Preparation time: 15 minutes, plus soaking
Cooking time: 1 hour 10 minutes

VARIATION

# Butter Bean Stew with Tomatoes and Rosemary

*The fresh rosemary adds a particularly aromatic and slightly exotic flavour to this rich tasting stew.*

4 tablespoons extra virgin olive oil,
   plus a little extra to drizzle
2 garlic cloves, crushed
1 tablespoon chopped fresh rosemary
2 teaspoons grated lemon rind
2 x 400 g/14 oz cans butter beans
4 large ripe tomatoes (about 750 g/
   1½ lb), peeled, deseeded and
   chopped
pinch of chilli powder
salt and pepper

**1** Heat the oil in a small frying pan, add the garlic, rosemary and lemon rind and fry gently for 3 minutes.
**2** Add the beans and their liquid, the tomatoes and a little chilli powder. Bring to the boil and simmer over a high heat for 8-10 minutes until the sauce is reduced and thickened. Taste and adjust the seasoning and serve at once.

**Serves 4**
Preparation time: 5 minutes
Cooking time: 10-12 minutes

## Crusted Cassoulet

*Cassoulet is the name of a classic southern French dish made with animal fats and beans. This vegetarian version is full of delicious flavours. I have added my own variation with a topping of sliced bread, spread with oil, garlic, thyme and grated cheese. It's a great dish for informal entertaining. Serve the cassoulet with a crisp green salad.*

125 g/4 oz dried haricot beans,
    soaked overnight
1.2 litres/2 pints water
15 g/½ oz dried ceps
150 ml/¼ pint boiling water
6 tablespoons extra virgin olive oil

2 garlic cloves, chopped
250 g/8 oz baby onions, halved
175 g/6 oz mixed mushrooms, sliced
1 tablespoon each chopped fresh
    thyme, rosemary and sage
2 carrots, diced
2 celery sticks, sliced
1 red pepper, deseeded and diced
150 ml/¼ pint red wine
4 tablespoons tomato purée
1 tablespoon dark soy sauce
salt and pepper

CRUST:
½ small French stick, sliced thinly
2 tablespoons extra virgin olive oil
1 garlic clove, crushed
2 tablespoons chopped fresh thyme
25 g/1 oz freshly grated vegetarian
    Parmesan cheese
salt and pepper

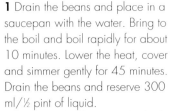

**1** Drain the beans and place in a saucepan with the water. Bring to the boil and boil rapidly for about 10 minutes. Lower the heat, cover and simmer gently for 45 minutes. Drain the beans and reserve 300 ml/½ pint of liquid.

**2** Soak the dried ceps in the boiling water for 20 minutes, then drain, reserving the liquid. Slice the ceps.

**3** Heat half the oil in a frying pan, fry the garlic and onions for 5 minutes. Add the mushrooms and herbs, stir-fry for a further 5 minutes until the mushrooms are golden.

**4** Heat the remaining oil in the frying pan and fry the carrots, celery and pepper for 5 minutes; add the wine and boil rapidly for 3 minutes. Stir in the reserved beans and their liquid, the mushroom mixture, tomato purée, reserved ceps and their liquid and soy sauce, season to taste. Spoon into 4 small or 1 large gratin dish.

**5** Slice the bread thinly and layer over the casserole. Mix the oil, garlic and thyme together, brush over the bread and scatter with the Parmesan. Cover loosely with foil and bake in a preheated oven, 190°C (375°F), Gas Mark 5, for 30 minutes. Remove the foil and bake for a further 20 minutes until the crust is golden.

**Serves 6**
Preparation time: 40 minutes,
plus soaking
Cooking time: 1½-1¾ hours
Oven temperature: 190°C (375°F),
Gas Mark 5

## Braised Soya Beans with Shiitake Mushrooms and Spinach

*This delightful combination of ingredients and flavours provides a tasty and nutritious dish. It is easy and quick to prepare and would make an ideal mid-week supper dish.*

175 g/6 oz soya beans,
   soaked overnight
3 tablespoons extra virgin olive oil
1 garlic clove, chopped
1 teaspoon grated root ginger
2 red chillies, deseeded and chopped
125 g/4 oz shiitake mushrooms, sliced
4 ripe tomatoes, skinned, deseeded
   and chopped
2 tablespoons dark soy sauce
2 tablespoons dry sherry
250 g/8 oz spinach leaves, washed
   and shredded

**1** Drain the beans and place in a saucepan with plenty of cold water. Bring to the boil and boil rapidly for 10 minutes, then lower the heat, cover and simmer for 1 hour or until the beans are tender. Drain, reserving 150 ml/¼ pint liquid.
**2** Heat the oil in a large frying pan, add the garlic, ginger and chillies and fry for 3 minutes. Add the mushrooms and fry for a further 5 minutes until tender.
**3** Add the tomatoes, beans, reserved liquid, soy sauce and sherry and bring to the boil. Cover and simmer for 15 minutes.
**4** Stir in the spinach and heat through for 2-3 minutes until the spinach is wilted. Serve at once.

**Serves 4**
Preparation time: 15 minutes, plus soaking
Cooking time: 1 hour 25 minutes

## *Basic Pizza Dough with Rosemary, Garlic and Olive Oil*

250 g/8 oz strong plain flour, plus extra for kneading
½ teaspoon salt
½ teaspoon fast-acting yeast (see page 7)
120 ml/4 fl oz warm water
1 tablespoon extra virgin olive oil, plus extra for oiling

TOPPING:

6 tablespoons extra virgin olive oil
3 garlic cloves, crushed
3 tablespoons chopped fresh rosemary
sea salt and pepper

**1** Sift the flour and salt into a large bowl and stir in the yeast. Make a well in the centre and gradually stir in the water and oil to form a soft dough.

**2** Turn out the dough on to a lightly floured surface and knead for 8-10 minutes until smooth and elastic. Place in an oiled bowl, turn the dough once to coat the surface with oil and cover with oiled clingfilm. Leave to rise in a warm place for 45 minutes or until doubled in size.

**3** Meanwhile, prepare the topping by combining all the ingredients together.

**4** Knead the risen dough lightly, divide in half and roll each piece out to a 23 cm/9 inch round. Transfer the rounds to 2 oiled pizza plates or a large oiled baking sheet. Prick the bases with a fork and carefully spread with the rosemary oil. Sprinkle over plenty of salt and pepper.

**5** Place at the top of a preheated oven, 220°C (425°F), Gas Mark 7, and bake for 15 minutes until lightly risen, crisp and golden. Serve at once.

**Makes 2 x 23 cm/9 inch pizzas**
Preparation time: 15 minutes, plus 45 minutes rising
Cooking time: 15 minutes
Oven temperature: 220°C (425°F), Gas Mark 7

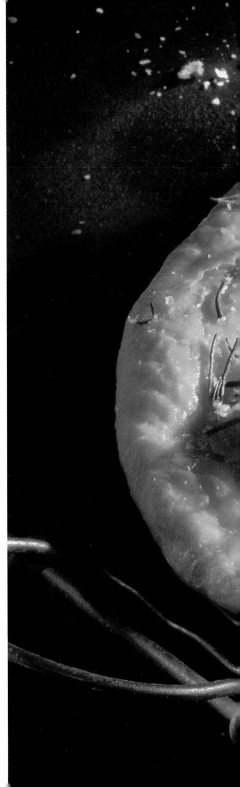

## Potato, Leek and Goats' Cheese Pizza Flan

*A tasty pizza dish cooked in a large flan tin giving extra depth to the flan.*

**1 quantity Basic Pizza Dough (see page 62)**
**vegetable oil, for oiling**
TOPPING:
**4 medium potatoes**
**2 tablespoons extra virgin olive oil, plus extra to drizzle**
**2 leeks, trimmed, cleaned and sliced**
**2 garlic cloves, chopped**
**1 tablespoon chopped fresh thyme**
**250 g/8 oz goats' cheese, sliced**
**25 g/1 oz pine nuts**
**salt and pepper**

**1** Prepare the dough according to the recipe on page 62 and leave to rise once. Place a baking sheet at the top of a preheated oven 230°C (450°F), Gas Mark 8.

**2** Cook the potatoes in salted boiling water for about 15 minutes until tender. Drain, refresh under cold water and then cut into slices. Heat the oil in a pan and fry the leeks and garlic for 5 minutes.

**3** Turn the dough out on to a lightly floured surface and knead gently for 1 minute. Roll the dough out and use to line an oiled 30 cm/12 inch flan tin, pressing the dough well up the sides of the tin. Prick the base well with a fork.

**4** Scatter the leeks, garlic and potatoes over the base and top with the thyme, goats' cheese, pine nuts and salt and pepper. Drizzle over a little extra oil if wished and bake on the preheated baking sheet for 10 minutes. Lower the temperature to 220°C (425°F), Gas Mark 7 and cook for a further 15 minutes until the topping is golden and bubbling.

**Serves 6-8**
Preparation time: 15 minutes, plus making dough and rising time
Cooking time: 45 minutes
Oven temperature: 230°C (450°F), Gas Mark 8, then 220°C (425°F), Gas Mark 7

## Onion and Sage Focaccia

15 g/½ oz fresh yeast (see page 7)
300 ml/½ pint warm water
300 g/10 oz strong plain flour, plus
    extra for dusting
pinch of sugar
175 g/6 oz fine semolina
1 teaspoon salt
4 tablespoons extra virgin olive oil, plus
    extra for oiling
1 tablespoon sea salt
½ onion, sliced
2 tablespoons sage, chopped

**1** Blend the yeast with half the warm water, 125 g/4 oz of flour and the sugar until evenly combined and leave in a warm place for about 10 minutes until frothy.
**2** Combine the remaining flour with the semolina and salt in a large bowl and gradually work in the frothed yeast, 2 tablespoons of the olive oil and enough of the remaining warm water to form a stiff dough. Knead for 8-10 minutes until smooth and elastic.
**3** Transfer to an oiled bowl, turning once to coat the dough, cover and leave to rise in a warm place until doubled in size, about 45 minutes. Knock back the dough on a lightly

floured surface by kneading gently. Shape or roll into a large flat oval and transfer to an oiled baking sheet.
**4** Heat the remaining 2 tablespoons of extra virgin olive oil in a frying pan and add the sliced onion and sage. Cook for 5 minutes until softened but not browned. Scatter over the dough with the sea salt. Bake in a preheated oven, 220°C (425°F), Gas Mark 7, for 30-35 minutes until risen and the bread sounds hollow when tapped on the bottom. Brush again with more oil.
**5** Cover the bread with a clean tea towel and place on a wire rack to cool. Serve still slightly warm or cold.

**Makes 1 flat loaf**
Preparation time: 10 minutes, plus making dough and rising time
Cooking time: 35 minutes
Oven temperature: 220°C (425°F), Gas Mark 7

**VARIATION**

## Olive Focaccia

Work 125 g/4 oz stoned and chopped black or green olives into the basic dough and continue as above leaving out the onion and sage topping.

# Many Tomato Pizza

1 quantity Basic Pizza Dough (see
    page 62)
extra virgin olive oil, for oiling and
    drizzling
TOPPING:
2 large ripe plum tomatoes, sliced
125 g/4 oz red cherry tomatoes,
    halved

125 g/4 oz yellow pear tomatoes,
    halved
4 sun-dried tomatoes in oil, drained
    and chopped roughly
handful of basil leaves, torn into pieces
2 teaspoons grated lemon rind
12 black olives, stoned
sea salt and pepper

**1** Make up the pizza dough according to the recipe on page 62 and leave
to rise once.
**2** Knead the dough lightly and divide into 2 equal pieces. Roll each piece of
dough out to a 23 cm/9 inch round and transfer to 2 oiled pizza plates or a
large oiled baking sheet.
**3** Dry the tomato slices on paper towels. Arrange all the tomatoes, the basil,
lemon rind and black olives over the pizzas. Season well and drizzle over a
little extra olive oil.
**4** Bake at the top of a preheated oven, 230°C (450°F), Gas Mark 8, for 20
minutes, until the bases are crisp and the top golden. Serve at once.

**Serves 4**
Preparation time: 10 minutes, plus making dough and rising time
Cooking time: 20 minutes
Oven temperature: 230°C (450°F), Gas Mark 8

VARIATION

# Pizza Margherita

1 quantity Basic Pizza Dough (see
    page 62)
TOPPING:
½ quantity Quick Tomato Sauce (see
    page 126)
300 g/10 oz mozzarella cheese,
    drained, dried and diced
12 stoned black olives (optional)
extra virgin olive oil, for oiling and
    drizzling

**1** Make up the dough according to
the recipe on page 62 and leave to
rise once.
**2** Knead the risen dough, divide in
half and roll each piece out to a
25 cm/10 inch round. Transfer to
2 oiled pizza plates or a large oiled
baking sheet.
**3** Divide the tomato sauce between
the 2 pizza bases and spread to
within 5 mm/¼ inch of the edge.
Sprinkle over the cheese and olives
and drizzle over a little oil.
**4** Place at the top of a preheated
oven, 230°C (450°F), Gas Mark
8 and bake for 20 minutes until bubbling and golden.

**Serves 2**
Preparation time: 10 minutes, plus
making dough and rising time
Cooking time: 20 minutes
Oven temperature: 230°C (450°F),
Gas Mark 8

68

## Walnut and Sultana Bread

15 g/½ oz fresh yeast
500 g/1 lb granary flour, plus extra for dusting
1 teaspoon sugar
300 ml/½ pint warm water
1 teaspoon salt
25 g/1 oz butter
50 g/2 oz organic oats, plus extra to sprinkle
50 g/2 oz walnuts, chopped roughly
50 g/2 oz sultanas
2 tablespoons malt extract
vegetable oil, for oiling

**1** Blend the yeast with 4 tablespoons of the flour, the sugar and half the water until well combined and leave in a warm place for 10 minutes until it is frothy.

**2** In a large bowl mix together the remaining flour and salt, rub in the butter and stir in the oats, nuts and sultanas. Make a well in the centre and gradually work in the frothed yeast, malt extract and remaining water to form a stiff dough.

**3** Turn out on to a lightly floured surface and knead for 8-10 minutes until the dough is smooth and elastic. Transfer to an oiled bowl, turning once to coat the dough with oil,

cover and leave to rise in a warm place for about 45 minutes or until doubled in size.

**4** Knock back the dough by gently kneading it once more, and shape into an oval loaf. Place the loaf on an oiled baking sheet, cover with oiled polythene and leave to rise for a further 20 minutes. Brush the surface of the loaf with water and scatter over extra oats.

**5** Slash the top several times and transfer to a preheated oven, 220°C (425°F), Gas Mark 7, for 35-40 minutes until risen and the bread sounds hollow when tapped on the bottom. Cool completely on a wire rack before slicing.

**Makes 1 large loaf**
Preparation time: 10 minutes, plus rising time
Cooking time: 40 minutes
Oven temperature: 220°C (425°F), Gas Mark 7

**VARIATION**

## Hazelnut and Apricot Bread

For a different flavour substitute an equal amount of hazelnuts and chopped ready-to-eat dried apricots for the walnuts and sultanas.

## Millet, Cheese and Cumin Loaf

50 g/2 oz millet
150 ml/¼ pint boiling water
15 g/½ oz fresh yeast
250 g/8 oz plain strong flour, plus
    extra for dusting
1 teaspoon sugar
150 ml/¼ pint warm water
250 g/8 oz wholemeal bread flour
2 teaspoons sea salt
1 teaspoon cumin seeds
125 g/4 oz vegetarian Cheddar
    cheese, grated
vegetable oil, for oiling

**1** Soak the millet in the boiling water for 20 minutes. Combine the yeast, 4 tablespoons of the plain flour and the sugar with the warm water in a small bowl and leave in a warm place for 10 minutes until frothy. Drain the millet and reserve any remaining liquid.

**2** In a large bowl mix together the remaining plain flour with the wholemeal flour, soaked millet, salt, cumin seeds and cheese. Make a well in the centre and gradually work in the frothed yeast, reserved millet liquid and enough extra warm water to form a stiff dough.

**3** Turn the dough out on to a lightly floured surface and knead for 8-10 minutes until smooth and elastic. Place in an oiled bowl, turning once to coat the dough, cover and leave to rise in a warm place for about 1 hour, or until doubled in size.

**4** Knock back the dough by kneading gently. Shape the dough into an oval and press into an oiled 1 kg/ 2 lb loaf tin. Brush the surface with a little oil and bake in a preheated oven, 230°C (450°F), Gas Mark 8, for 35-40 minutes until risen and golden. The bread should sound hollow when tapped lightly on the bottom. Cool completely on a wire rack before slicing.

**Makes 1 x 1 kg/2 lb loaf**
Preparation time: 15 minutes, plus rising time
Cooking time: 35 minutes
Oven temperature: 230°C (450°F), Gas Mark 8

**VARIATION**

## Caraway and Fresh Herb Bread

Substitute caraway seeds for the cumin seeds and add 2 tablespoons chopped fresh herbs, for an equally delicious and unusual bread.

## Spinach and Chickpea Flan

1 quantity Shortcrust Pastry (see page 76)
butter, for greasing
FILLING:
175 g/6 oz fresh spinach leaves
2 tablespoons extra virgin olive oil
1 small onion, sliced thinly
2 garlic cloves, crushed
1 teaspoon ground turmeric
200 g/7 oz canned chickpeas, drained
2 eggs, lightly beaten
200 ml/7 fl oz single cream
pinch of grated nutmeg
salt and pepper

**1** Make the pastry, wrap and chill for 30 minutes. Roll out on a lightly floured surface, use to line a greased deep 20 cm/8 inch flluted flan tin. Prick the base, chill for 20 minutes. Line with foil and baking beans and bake in a preheated oven, 200°C (400°F), Gas Mark 6, for 10 minutes. Remove foil and beans, bake for a further 10-12 minutes until the pastry is crisp and golden.
**2** Meanwhile, prepare the filling. Wash the spinach leaves and place in a large pan. Heat gently for 3-4 minutes until the spinach is just wilted, drain well and squeeze out all the excess liquid. Chop finely and set aside.
**3** Heat the oil in a pan, add onion, garlic and turmeric, fry for 5 minutes, stir in the chickpeas and spinach remove from heat. Spread over the pastry case.
**4** Beat tthe eggs, cream, nutmeg and seasoning together and pour into the pastry case. Bake for 35-40 minutes until firm and golden.

**Serves 6-8**
Preparation time: 15 minutes, plus making pastry and chilling time
Cooking time: 1 hour-1 hour 10 minutes
Oven temperature: 200°C (400°F), Gas Mark 6

# Mediterranean Suet Parcel

*The texture of this suet pastry is particularly good: crisp on the outside with a light fluffy centre. The vegetable filling can be prepared in advance.*

**500 g/1 lb self-raising flour**
**1 teaspoon salt**
**175 g/6 oz vegetable suet**
**150 ml/¼ pint natural yogurt**
**200 ml/7 fl oz milk**
FILLING:
**2 aubergines**
**2 tablespoons extra virgin olive oil**
**2 large red peppers, cored, deseeded and quartered**
**4 firm ripe tomatoes, sliced**
**12 large basil leaves**
**175 g/6 oz mozzarella cheese, sliced thinly**
**Egg glaze (see page 9)**
**Mushroom Gravy (see page 127), to serve**

**1** Sift the flour and salt into a large bowl, stir in the suet and then gradually work in the yogurt and milk to form a stiff dough. Knead lightly until smooth, wrap and leave to rest while preparing the filling.
**2** Thickly slice the aubergines lengthways, brush with a little oil and grill for 5-6 minutes on each side until golden and tender. Grill the pepper quarters for 6-8 minutes until charred and tender, wrap in a plastic bag and leave until cool enough to handle. Peel off the skin.
**3** Roll out the dough on a lightly floured surface to a 35 cm/14 inch square. Arrange the aubergines, peppers, tomatoes, basil and cheese in layers, diagonally in the centre of the square, forming a 20 cm/8 inch square shape.
**4** Dampen the edges of the pastry with a little water and draw up the 4 corners, pressing together in the middle to seal in the filling.
**5** Transfer the parcel to a baking sheet, brush with glaze and bake in a preheated oven, 200°C (400°F). Gas Mark 6, for 30 minutes. Lower the temperature to 180°C (350°F), Gas Mark 4, and bake for a further 15 minutes until puffed up and golden. Rest for 5 minutes and serve hot with mushroom gravy and a green salad.

**Serves 6**
Preparation time: 40 minutes, plus making mushroom gravy
Cooking time: 1 hour
Oven temperature: 200°C (400°F), Gas Mark 4

# Savoury Bread Tart

*This bread tart is what I call real comfort food – a savoury version of the classic bread and butter pudding.*

1 small French stick
vegetable oil, for oiling
3 eggs, lightly beaten
450 ml/¾ pint milk
pinch of cayenne pepper
2 tablespoons chopped fresh chives
50 g/2 oz freshly grated vegetarian
   Parmesan cheese
salt and pepper

**1** Slice the French stick fairly thinly and arrange in overlapping rounds in an oiled capacity baking dish.
**2** Whisk the eggs, milk, cayenne, chives, half the cheese and the salt and pepper together and pour over the bread. Press the bread down well into the mixture. Top with the remaining Parmesan cheese and bake in a preheated oven, 170°C (325°F), Gas Mark 3, for 45 minutes until puffed up and golden and firm in the centre.

**Serves 4**
Preparation time: 5 minutes
Cooking time: 45-50 minutes
Oven temperature: 170°C (325°F), Gas Mark 3

# Rich Vegetable Pie in Flaky Pastry

*This is the dish I cook when I feel the need for a rich savoury pie.*

1 quantity Flaky Pastry (see right)
4 tablespoons extra virgin olive oil
500 g/1 lb button mushrooms, halved
2 garlic cloves, crushed
250 g/8 oz baby onions, halved
250 g/8 oz parsnips, chopped
250 g/8 oz carrots, chopped
2 tablespoons chopped fresh thyme
1 tablespoon chopped fresh sage

300 ml/½ pint full-bodied dry red wine
1 x 400 g/14 oz can chopped tomatoes
150 ml/¼ pint Vegetable Stock (see page 126)
2 tablespoons tomato purée
2 tablespoons dark soy sauce
Egg Glaze (see page 9)
salt and pepper

**1** Prepare and make the flaky pastry according to the recipe on the right and chill for 30 minutes.
**2** Make the filling. Heat half the oil in a pan, add the mushrooms and garlic and stir-fry for 3-4 minutes until golden. Remove from the pan and set aside.
**3** Add the remaining oil to the pan and fry the onions, parsnips, carrots and herbs for 10 minutes until golden. Add the wine and boil rapidly for 3 minutes. Stir in the tomatoes, stock, tomato purée and soy sauce. Bring to the boil, cover and simmer for 30 minutes.
**4** Add the mushrooms to the stew, season to taste, transfer to a 1.75 litre/ 3 pint pie dish and set aside.
**5** Roll out the pastry on a lightly floured surface, to a little larger than the pie dish. Cut 4 strips 2.5 cm/1 inch wide from around the edge of the pastry and press on to the rim of the pie dish, wetting the rim as you go.
**6** Carefully lay the remaining pastry over the top of the pie, trim the edges with a knife to fit and press together well, again wetting the pastry to seal. Flute the edges and use any trimmings to make leaf shapes to decorate the top of the pie.
**7** Brush the pastry with egg glaze and bake in a preheated oven, 220°C (425°F), Gas Mark 7, for 20 minutes, then lower the temperature to 200°C (400°F), Gas Mark 6, and bake for a further 15 minutes.

**Serves 6**
Preparation time: 30 minutes, plus making pastry and chilling time
Cooking time: 1 hour 20 minutes
Oven temperature: 220°C (425°F), Gas Mark 7, then 200°C (400°F), Gas Mark 6

# Flaky Pastry

200 g/7 oz plain white flour
1 teaspoon salt
125 g/4 oz butter or hard vegetable margarine
100 ml/3½ fl oz cold water

**1** Sift the flour and salt into a bowl and rub in 25 g/1 oz of the butter or margarine. Gradually work in the water to form a soft dough. Turn out on to a lightly floured surface and knead gently until smooth.
**2** Roll out the dough to an oblong about 5 mm/¼ inch thick. Dot 25 g/1 oz of the remaining butter or margarine over two-thirds of the surface of the dough, folding the uncovered third back over half the covered dough and finally the remaining dough back over that, enclosing all the butter.
**3** Seal the edges by pressing firmly with the rolling pin. Turn the dough once to the left and roll out to an oblong again. Repeat the whole process, then wrap and chill for 10 minutes.
**4** Repeat the dotting and folding one final time and then re-roll a further 2 times without butter. Wrap and chill the dough for at least 30 minutes before using.

**Makes 450 g/14 oz pastry**
Preparation time: 20 minutes, plus chilling time

## Courgette, Sun-dried Tomato and Ricotta Flan

*Ricotta is an Italian whey cheese with a creamy texture and mild flavour. Curd cheese can be substituted but use ricotta if possible for its superior texture and taste.*

1 quantity Shortcrust Pastry (see right)
2 tablespoons extra virgin olive oil, plus extra for oiling
1 small onion, sliced thinly
2 courgettes, sliced thinly
50 g/2 oz drained sun-dried tomatoes in oil, sliced
250 g/8 oz ricotta or curd cheese
2 tablespoons milk
2 eggs, beaten
4 tablespoons chopped fresh herbs (basil, rosemary, sage, thyme)
12 stoned black olives, halved
salt and pepper

**1** Make the pastry according to the recipe on the right, wrap and chill for 30 minutes. Roll out the dough on a lightly floured surface and use to line an oiled 23 cm/9 inch fluted flan tin. Prick the base and chill for a further 20 minutes.
**2** Line the pastry case with foil and baking beans and bake in a pre-heated oven, 200°C (400°F), Gas Mark 6, for 10 minutes. Remove the foil and beans, bake for 10-12

minutes until the pastry is golden.
**3** Heat the oil in a frying pan, add the onion and courgettes and fry gently for 5-6 minutes until lightly golden. Scatter over the base of the pastry case and top with the sun-dried tomatoes.
**4** Beat the ricotta, milk, eggs, herbs and salt and pepper together and spread over the courgette mixture. Scatter over the olives and return to the oven for a further 30-35 minutes until firm and golden.

Serves 6-8
Preparation time: 20 minutes, plus making pastry and chilling time
Cooking time: 55-60 minutes
Oven temperature: 200°C (400°F), Gas Mark 6

## Shortcrust Pastry

175 g/6 oz plain flour, plus extra for dusting
½ teaspoon salt
75 g/3 oz butter, diced
2-3 tablespoons cold water

**1** Sift the flour and salt into a bowl, rub in the butter until the mixture resembles fine breadcrumbs. Gradually work in enough water to form a soft dough.
**2** Knead the dough on a lightly floured surface until smooth, wrap in clingfilm and chill for 30 minutes. Use as required.

Makes 300 g/10 oz pastry, enough to line a 23-25 cm/9-10 inch flan tin

# Asparagus, Walnut and Parmesan Quiche

*The egg custard is enriched with a garlic purée adding a wonderfully mellow flavour without overpowering the asparagus.*

**1 quantity Shortcrust Pastry (see left)**
**butter, for greasing**
FILLING:
**10 whole garlic cloves peeled**
**2 tablespoons extra virgin olive oil**
**375 g/12 oz asparagus spears**
**40 g/1½ oz walnuts, toasted and chopped**
**200 ml/7 fl oz single cream or milk**
**3 eggs, lightly beaten**
**75 g/3 oz freshly grated vegetarian Parmesan cheese**
**salt and pepper**

**1** Make the pastry according to the recipe on the left, wrap and chill for 30 minutes. Roll out the pastry on a lightly floured surface and use to line a greased deep 23 cm/9 inch fluted flan tin. Prick the base with a fork and chill for a 20 minutes.
**2** Meanwhile, cook the garlic cloves in boiling water for 10 minutes, drain well and pat dry. Mash with 1 tablespoon of the oil to form a paste.
**3** Line the flan with foil and baking beans and bake in a preheated oven, 200°C (400°F), Gas Mark 6,

for 10 minutes. Remove the foil and beans and bake for a further 10-12 minutes until the pastry is crisp and golden. Lower the temperature to 190°C (375°F), Gas Mark 5.
**4** Heat the remaining oil and stir-fry the asparagus spears for 5 minutes. Scatter over the pastry case with the walnuts. Beat together the cream or milk, garlic paste, eggs, Parmesan and salt and pepper, pour over the asparagus and bake for 25 minutes until set and golden.

**Serves 6-8**
Preparation time: 15 minutes, plus making pastry and chilling time
Cooking time: 50 minutes, including pastry case
Oven temperature: 200°C (400°F) Gas Mark 6 then 190°C (375°F), Gas Mark 5

## *Roasted Vegetable and Bread Salad*

1 large aubergine, cubed
4 courgettes, cubed
2 red peppers, cored, deseeded and sliced
4 whole peeled garlic cloves
extra virgin olive oil
4 firm ripe tomatoes, diced
175 g/6 oz day-old bread, diced
2 tablespoons boiling water
4 tablespoons chopped fresh basil

DRESSING:

9 tablespoons extra virgin olive oil
2 tablespoon red wine vinegar
pinch of sugar
3 tablespoons boiling water
salt and pepper

**1** Toss the aubergine, courgettes, peppers and garlic cloves with about 4 tablespoons of olive oil and place in a large roasting pan. Bake in a preheated oven, 220°C (425°F), Gas Mark 7, for 50 minutes.

**2** Remove the pan from the oven and in stir the tomatoes with a little extra oil if necessary. Whisk the dressing ingredients together, except for the water. Stir 3 tablespoons of the dressing into the vegetables and leave to cool.

**3** Place the bread in a bowl. Add the boiling water to the remaining dressing and stir into the bread, then leave to soak for 10 minutes. Just before serving add the bread to the vegetables with the basil and season to taste. Transfer to a serving dish and serve at room temperature.

**Serves 4**
Preparation time: 25 minutes, plus cooling time
Cooking time: 50 minutes
Oven temperature: 220°C (425°F), Gas Mark 7

# Mesclun with Croûtons and Cheese Dressing

*Mesclun is a French salad using wild salad leaves and grasses. This simple salad is tossed with a tangy cheese dressing: I often serve it as a summer starter.*

250 g/8 oz mixed salad leaves
25 g/1 oz flat-leaf parsley
4 thick slices day-old white bread
1 large garlic clove

DRESSING:

25 g/1 oz dolcelatte cheese, softened
25 g/1 oz ricotta cheese, softened
6 tablespoons extra virgin olive oil
1 tablespoon white wine vinegar
1 tablespoon boiling water

**salt and pepper**

**1** Wash all the salad leaves and the parsley, shake off the excess water and transfer to a plastic bag. Wrap and chill for 30 minutes.

**2** To make the dressing, blend the 2 cheeses together and gradually beat in the oil, vinegar, boiling water and salt and pepper to form a smooth thick sauce.

**3** Transfer the salad leaves to a large bowl. Toast the bread lightly on both sides and while still warm, rub all over with the garlic. Cut the bread into cubes.

**4** Pour the dressing over the salad leaves, toss well and serve at once.

**Serves 4**
Preparation time: 10 minutes, plus 30 minutes chilling
Cooking time: 2-3 minutes

## Bitter Salad with Sweet Maple and Chive Dressing

125 g/4 oz frisée or escarole
2 small heads chicory
1 small head radicchio
50 g/2 oz rocket leaves
chive flowers, to garnish

DRESSING:

5 tablespoons extra virgin olive or nut oil
1 tablespoon raspberry or red wine vinegar
2 tablespoons chopped fresh chives
1 teaspoon maple syrup
salt and pepper

**1** Wash the frisée and tear into bite-sized pieces. Slice the chicory and radicchio and wash well with the rocket leaves. Shake off all the excess water from the leaves transfer to a plastic bag. Chill for 30 minutes.
**2** Make up the dressing. Place all the ingredients in a screw-top jar and shake well until amalgamated.
**3** Put the salad leaves into a bowl, shake the dressing again and pour over the salad. Toss well and serve garnished with chive flowers.

### Serves 4-6
Preparation time: 5 minutes, plus 30 minutes chilling

# Country Salad with Horseradish Dressing

*A cornucopia of typical garden vegetables combine to make a satisfying and robust salad. When hard-boiling the eggs, carefully spoon them into a pan of gently simmering water. Return to the boil and cook for 8 minutes. Drain and plunge into cold water. Peel and quarter when required.*

250 g/8 oz shelled broad beans
125 g/4 oz green beans, halved
500 g/1 lb firm ripe plum tomatoes
½ small cucumber, sliced thickly
2 celery sticks, sliced
175 g/6 oz cooked beetroot, sliced
1 small red onion, sliced thinly
2 tablespoons drained capers
2 soft, hard-boiled eggs, peeled and
   halved
salt

DRESSING:
2 tablespoons grated horseradish or
   1 tablespoon creamed horseradish
4 tablespoons extra virgin olive oil
2 teaspoons red wine vinegar
pinch of sugar
2 tablespoons chopped fresh herbs

**1** Blanch the broad beans in boiling, salted water for 1 minute, drain, refresh under cold water and pat dry on paper towels. Peel and discard the tough outer skin. Blanch the green beans for 1 minute, drain, refresh under cold water and pat dry on paper towels.
**2** Place the beans in a large bowl and add the tomatoes, cucumber, celery, beetroot, onion and capers.
**3** Place all the dressing ingredients in a bowl and whisk together until evenly combined. Pour over the salad and toss well until all the ingredients are evenly coated. Transfer the salad to a serving dish and top with the egg halves. Serve at once.

**Serves 4**
Preparation time: 20 minutes
Cooking time: 10 minutes

# Greek Style Country Salad

1 kg/2 lb beefsteak tomatoes, chopped
1 small sweet green pepper, deseeded
   and sliced
½ red onion, sliced
125 g/4 oz cucumber, sliced
2 teaspoons of oregano
125 g/4 oz feta cheese
DRESSING:
6 tablespoons extra virgin olive oil
1 tablespoon lemon juice
salt and pepper

**1** Arrange the tomatoes, pepper, onion and cucumber on 4 serving plates and scatter over the oregano.
**2** Cut the cheese into 4 slabs and place 1 on to each salad. Combine the dressing ingredients together, drizzle over the salads and serve at once.

**Serves 4**
Preparation time: 5 minutes

# Spicy Cauliflower, Lentil and Pepper Salad

*Puy lentils are available from health food stores and have a lovely nutty flavour. If unavailable brown lentils are a good alternative.*

125 g/4 oz Puy lentils, rinsed
2 large peppers, cored, deseeded and quartered
3 tablespoons extra virgin olive oil
375 g/12 oz cauliflower florets, halved if large
2 teaspoons chilli flakes
1 garlic clove, crushed
1 tablespoon grated lemon rind
50 g/2 oz stoned black olives, halved
salt

DRESSING:
4 tablespoons extra virgin olive oil
2 tablespoons Red Pesto (see page 126)
2 tablespoons chopped fresh parsley
2 teaspoons balsamic vinegar
salt and pepper
parsley sprigs to garnish

**1** Place the rinsed lentils in a pan with plenty of cold water. Bring to the boil, boil rapidly for 10 minutes, then simmer gently for 30 minutes, until tender. Drain, refresh under cold water, drain again.

**2** Meanwhile, brush the peppers with a little of the oil and cook under a hot grill for 6-8 minutes on each side until tender and charred. Transfer to a plastic bag and set aside until cool enough to handle. Peel off the skin and slice the flesh.

**3** Blanch the cauliflower florets in boiling, salted water for 1 minute, drain, refresh under cold water, dry on paper towels. Heat the oil in a pan, add the chilli flakes, garlic and lemon rind, fry gently for 3 minutes. Add the cauliflower florets, and stir-fry for 3-4 minutes until tender.

**4** Blend all the dressing ingredients together. Transfer the cauliflower mixture to a large bowl, stir in the lentils, peppers and the dressing and toss until well coated. Serve at once garnished with parsley sprigs.

**Serves 4**
Preparation time: 20 minutes, plus making pesto
Cooking time: 40 minutes

## Tomato and Coriander Salad

1 kg/2 lb mixed tomatoes, sliced or
   quartered, use yellow cherry
   tomatoes if available
2 teaspoons grated lime rind
½ small red onion, sliced thinly
1 tablespoon sesame seeds, toasted
   (optional)

DRESSING:

2 tablespoons chopped fresh coriander
1 tablespoon lime juice
1 garlic clove, crushed
½ teaspoon clear honey
pinch of cayenne pepper
4 tablespoons extra virgin olive oil
salt and pepper

**1** First make the dressing. Whisk
together the coriander, lime juice,
garlic, honey, cayenne and salt and
pepper and then whisk in the oil.
**2** Arrange the tomatoes in a large
serving bowl and scatter over the
lime rind, onion and toasted sesame
seeds, if using.
**3** Whisk the dressing ingredients
once more and pour over the salad.
Cover the salad and set aside for
30 minutes for the flavours to
develop, before serving.

**Serves 4**
Preparation time: 5 minutes, plus
30 minutes marinating

# Noodle Salad with Mung Beans

*Noodles work equally well cold or hot, but when they are served cold they do need plenty of dressing or they can become rather dry. Frying the basil leaves until crispy is typical of Thai cooking on which this recipe is based.*

50 g/2 oz dried mung beans,
   soaked overnight
6 tablespoons sunflower oil
1 garlic clove, crushed
1 teaspoon grated root ginger
2 tablespoons light soy sauce
1 tablespoon lime juice

pinch of cayenne pepper
50 g/2 oz dried thread egg noodles
125 g/4 oz carrots, sliced thinly
1 small red pepper, cored, deseeded
   and sliced thinly
125 g/4 oz asparagus tips
15 g/½ oz basil leaves

**1** Drain the beans and place in a saucepan with plenty of cold water. Bring to the boil and boil rapidly for 10 minutes. Lower the heat and simmer gently for 35-40 minutes until tender.

**2** Whisk together 4 tablespoons of the oil, the garlic, ginger, soy sauce, lime juice and cayenne. Drain the cooked beans and toss with half the dressing. Set aside to cool.

**3** Cook the noodles according to the packet instructions. Drain, refresh under cold water and then toss with the remaining dressing.

**4** Heat half the remaining oil in a frying pan and stir-fry the vegetables for 2-3 minutes until just tender, then transfer to a large bowl. Add the remaining oil to the pan and fry the basil leaves for 1-2 minutes until crisp and golden. Drain on paper towels.

**5** Arrange the noodles on serving plates. Toss the mung beans with the vegetables and spoon over the noodles. Top with the crispy basil leaves and serve at once.

**Serves 4**
Preparation time: 20 minutes, plus soaking time
Cooking time: 55-60 minutes

## New Potato and French Bean Salad with Basil Mayonnaise

*Frying the cooked potatoes adds depth of flavour, although the more health-conscious may omit this step.*

500 g/1 lb new potatoes
2 tablespoons extra virgin olive oil
175 g/6 oz French beans
50 g/2 oz stoned black olives
6 ripe plum tomatoes, sliced
1 small leek, trimmed, cleaned and
   shredded thinly
salt

BASIL MAYONNAISE:

3 tablespoons Classic Mayonnaise (see
   page 127)
15 g/½ oz basil leaves, finely chopped
1 small garlic clove, crushed
½ teaspoon lemon juice
1 tablespoon extra virgin olive oil
1 tablespoon boiling water
salt and pepper

**1** Cook the new potatoes in boiling, salted water for 10 minutes until just tender. Drain, refresh under cold running water and pat dry on paper towels. Cut the potatoes in half or quarters if large.
**2** Heat the oil in a frying pan, add the potatoes and fry gently for 4-5 minutes until evenly golden. Drain and set aside to cool.

**3** Blanch the beans in boiling, salted water for 2 minutes until just tender, drain, refresh under cold water and pat dry.
**4** Make the dressing. Put the mayonnaise in a bowl, beat in the remaining ingredients until evenly combined. Adjust seasoning.
**5** Put the potatoes, beans and olives in a bowl and stir in enough dressing to lightly coat the vegetables.

Arrange the sliced tomatoes on a serving plate, spoon over the potato and bean mixture and scatter the shredded leeks on top. Serve at once.

**Serves 4**
Preparation time: 10 minutes, plus making mayonnaise
Cooking time: 17 minutes

# Artichoke and Water Chestnut Salad

*Canned artichoke hearts and water chestnuts are put to good use in this delightful salad, inspired by a local bistro that consistently provides exciting combinations of ingredients.*

125 g/4 oz watercress
125 g/4 oz baby spinach leaves
½ small frisée lettuce
1 x 400 g/14 oz can cooked artichoke
   hearts, drained and sliced
1 x 227 g/7½ oz can water chestnuts,
   drained and sliced
1 large firm, ripe pear, peeled,
   quartered, cored and thinly sliced
25 g/1 oz flaked almonds, toasted
DRESSING:
3 tablespoons groundnut oil
2 teaspoons sesame oil
1 tablespoon light soy sauce
1 tablespoon sherry vinegar
½ teaspoon clear honey
pepper

**1** Trim and discard any thick stalks from the watercress, wash carefully along with the spinach and frisée. Tear the frisée into bite-sized pieces and shake off the excess water from all the leaves. Transfer to a plastic bag, seal and chill for 30 minutes.
**2** Place the leaves in a large bowl with the artichokes and water chestnuts. Add the pear to the salad with the almonds.
**3** Mix all the dressing ingredients together until blended, then pour over the salad. Toss well to coat the leaves and serve immediately.

**Serves 4**
Preparation time: 15 minutes, plus
   chilling time

# Marinated Mushroom Salad with Straw Potatoes

*The straw potatoes add some bite to this delicious marinated mushroom salad. The mushrooms need to marinate long enough for the dressing to soften them.*

500 g/1 lb flat mushrooms
double quantity Balsamic Dressing
  (see right)
250 g/8 oz potatoes

vegetable oil, for frying
125 g/4 oz salad leaves
6 spring onions, sliced thinly
salt and pepper

**1** Wipe the mushrooms with a damp cloth and then slice them very thinly. Place on a large plate. Whisk together the dressing (see right) and pour half over the mushrooms. Set aside for 1 hour, turning occasionally until softened.
**2** Peel the potatoes and then cut into very thin matchsticks. Heat 1 cm/½ inch oil in a frying pan and fry the potato straws for 2-3 minutes until crisp and golden. Drain on paper towels.
**3** Wash and dry the salad leaves, toss with the remaining dressing, then place on serving plates. Arrange the marinated mushrooms on the leaves and top with the spring onions and finally the straw potatoes. Serve at once.

**Serves 4**
Preparation time: 15 minutes
Cooking time: 2-3 minutes

# French Dressing

*There are so many variations of a classic French dressing or vinaigrette, but here is my own favourite.*

1 tablespoon white or red wine vinegar
1 teaspoon Dijon mustard
pinch of sugar
6 tablespoons extra virgin olive oil
salt and pepper

Put the vinegar, mustard, sugar and salt and pepper into a small bowl and whisk well. Gradually whisk in the oil until well blended.

**Makes approximately 100 ml/3½ fl oz**

VARIATIONS

## Balsamic Dressing

Whisk together 2 teaspoons balsamic vinegar, 2 teaspoons wholegrain mustard, salt and pepper and then gradually whisk in 5 tablespoons extra virgin olive oil until blended.

## Herb Dressing

Add 2 tablespoons chopped fresh herbs (such as chives, basil, tarragon, chervil, parsley) to the above dressing.

# Warm Fennel and Red Pepper Caponata

*This warm salad is based on the classic Sicilian caponata, a sweet/savoury stew of aubergines, peppers, olives and raisins. It is made here with fennel, my favourite vegetable.*

4 tablespoons extra virgin olive oil
3 heads fennel, sliced thinly
1 small onion, sliced
3 red peppers, cored, deseeded and
   sliced
4 garlic cloves, sliced
1 tablespoon chopped fresh rosemary
1 tablespoon chopped fresh thyme
150 ml/¼ pint white wine
500 g/1 lb ripe tomatoes, skinned,
   deseeded and diced or 1 x 400 g/
   14 oz can chopped tomatoes
50 g/2 oz stoned green olives
25 g/1 oz capers
50 g/2 oz blanched almonds, toasted
4 tablespoons chopped parsley

**1** Heat half the oil in a large deep frying pan or skillet, fry the fennel in batches for 6-8 minutes until golden on both sides. Remove from the pan with a slotted spoon and set aside.
**2** Add the remaining oil to the pan and fry the onion, peppers, garlic, rosemary and thyme for 5 minutes. Pour in the wine and boil rapidly for 3 minutes.

**3** Return the fennel to the pan with the tomatoes, bring to the boil, cover and simmer for 20 minutes. Add the remaining ingredients to the pan and cook for a further 10-15 minutes until the vegetables are tender. Cool to room temperature and serve with crusty bread and a green salad.

**Serves 4**
Preparation time: 15 minutes, plus cooling time
Cooking time: 45-50 minutes

# Carrots with Ginger and Orange Butter

*A really simple way of spicing up carrots.*

**1 kg/2 lb carrots, sliced or whole baby carrots**

GINGER AND ORANGE BUTTER:
**50 g/2 oz butter, softened**
**1 teaspoon grated root ginger**
**½ teaspoon grated orange rind**
**½ tablespoon orange juice**
**½ teaspoon clear honey**
**1 tablespoon chopped fresh chervil**
**salt and pepper**

**1** Steam or boil the carrots for 10-12 minutes until tender.
**2** Meanwhile, make the ginger and orange butter. Place all the ingredients in a food processor and blend until smooth and evenly combined.
**3** Transfer the cooked carrots to a warmed serving dish, add the butter and toss well together until the carrots are thoroughly coated with the butter. Serve at once.

**Serves 4-6**
Preparation time: 10 minutes
Cooking time: 10-15 minutes

# Roasted Autumn Vegetables, with a Garlic Sauce

*Roasting vegetables in a hot oven draws out their natural sweetness and intense flavour. It is important to cut the vegetables into similar-size pieces so they cook evenly.*

1 large head garlic
2 large onions, cut into wedges
8 small carrots, quartered
8 small parsnips
12 small potatoes, halved if large
2 head fennel, sliced thickly
4 rosemary sprigs
4 thyme sprigs
6 tablespoons extra virgin olive oil

GARLIC SAUCE:
1 large slice of day-old bread (about 75 g/3 oz)
4 tablespoons milk
75 ml/3 fl oz extra virgin olive oil
salt and pepper

**1** Blanch the whole head of garlic in boiling water for 5 minutes. Drain and pat dry on paper towels.

**2** Put all the vegetables and herbs in a large roasting pan, placing the garlic in the middle. Season well and stir in the oil to coat the vegetables. Cover the tin with foil and bake in a preheated oven, 220°C (425°F), Gas Mark 7, for 50 minutes. Remove the foil and bake for a further 30 minutes.

**3** Remove the head of garlic. Carefully peel and discard the skin and mash the garlic flesh with a fork. Put the bread in a bowl, add the milk and soak for 5 minutes.

**4** Place the bread and garlic flesh in a blender and process to form a smooth paste. Gradually blend in the oil a little at a time until evenly combined and season to taste.

**5** Serve the roasted vegetables accompanied by the garlic sauce to dip.

**Serves 4-6**
Preparation time: 25 minutes
Cooking time: 1 hour 25 minutes
Oven temperature: 220°C (425°F), Gas Mark 7

VARIATION

# Roasted Onions with Balsamic Vinegar

6 large red onions
3 tablespoons extra virgin olive oil
1 tablespoon chopped fresh thyme
1 tablespoon chopped fresh rosemary
2 garlic cloves, crushed
1 teaspoon coriander seeds, crushed
4 tablespoons balsamic vinegar
4 tablespoons red wine
1 tablespoon clear honey
salt and pepper

**1** Slice the onions into eighths from the stalk to the root without cutting all the way through and press open. Place in a roasting pan.

**2** Combine the oil, herbs, garlic, coriander seeds and seasoning. Drizzle over the onions and bake in a preheated oven, 220°C (425°F), Gas Mark 7, for 30 minutes.

**3** Mix the vinegar, wine and honey together, pour a little over each onion and bake for a further 25-30 minutes until the onions are tender. Serve with the glazed juices.

**Serves 6**
Preparation time: 10 minutes
Cooking time: 1 hour
Oven temperature: 220°C (425°F), Gas Mark 7

## Mixed Bean Sauté with Almonds and Chives

**750 g/1½ lb mixed beans, trimmed and sliced as necessary (broad beans, runner beans, French beans, flat beans, yellow string beans etc.)**
**2 tablespoons almond or extra virgin olive oil**
**1 small leek, trimmed, cleaned and sliced**
**2 garlic cloves, sliced**
**50 g/2 oz flaked almonds**
**2 tablespoons chopped fresh chives**
**salt and pepper**

**1** Blanch all the beans together in a large pan of lightly salted, boiling water for 1 minute. Drain, refresh under cold water and pat dry on paper towels.
**2** Heat the oil in a wok or large frying pan, add the leek, garlic and almonds and fry gently for 3 minutes until softened. Add the beans, stir-fry for 3-4 minutes until tender and then stir in the chives and salt and pepper. Serve immediately.

**Serves 4**
Preparation time: 30 minutes
Cooking time: 8-10 minutes

# Leeks Baked with Blue Cheese and Hazelnuts

*The emphasis on this dish is simplicity. The leeks are baked with a little stock to soften them and are then roasted with the addition of the cheese and nuts.*

750 g/1½ lb baby leeks, trimmed, cleaned and halved
2 tablespoons hazelnut oil
4 tablespoons vegetable stock
15 g/½ oz butter
125 g/4 oz dolcelatte cheese, crumbled
2 tablespoons hazelnuts, chopped
2 tablespoons chopped fresh chervil
salt and pepper

**1** Toss the leeks with the oil and place in a large roasting pan with the stock. Bake in a preheated oven, 200°C (400°F), Gas Mark 6, for 15 minutes. Remove the pan from the oven.
**2** Dot with the butter, cheese, nuts and chervil, return to the oven and cook for a further 15-20 minutes until the leeks are tender and the cheese melted and golden. Season and serve immediately.

**Serves 4-6**
Preparation time: 5 minutes
Cooking time: 35-40 minutes
Oven temperature: 200°C (400°F), Gas Mark 6

# Roasted Jerusalem Artichokes

*The Jerusalem artichoke is a very underrated vegetable, perhaps due to its anonymity: it could easily be mistaken for just another variety of the potato family. However, it has a flavour all of its own – somewhere between turnip and potato with a nutty, almost peppery taste. When cooking by this method, there is no need to peel the artichokes.*

750 g/1½ lb Jerusalem artichokes, scrubbed
4 tablespoons walnut or extra virgin olive oil
12 whole garlic cloves
1 tablespoon chopped fresh sage
25 g/1 oz walnuts, toasted and chopped
salt and pepper

**1** Cut any larger artichokes in half so they are all roughly the same size and blanch in lightly salted boiling water for 5 minutes.
**2** Drain well and immediately toss with the oil, garlic, sage and salt and pepper. Place in a roasting pan and bake in a preheated oven, 200°C (400°F), Gas Mark 6, for 30 minutes, turning occasionally until golden and tender.
**3** Transfer to a warmed serving dish, scatter over the chopped walnuts and serve at once.

**Serves 4**
Preparation time: 10 minutes
Cooking time: 30 minutes
Oven temperature: 200°C (400°F), Gas Mark 6

VARIATION

# Roasted Parsnips with Thyme Butter

625 g/1¼ lb baby parsnips, scrubbed
1 tablespoon extra virgin olive oil
1 garlic clove, crushed
2 thyme sprigs, bruised
THYME BUTTER:
25 g/1 oz butter
1 tablespoon chopped fresh thyme
1 teaspoon grated lemon rind
pinch of cayenne pepper
pinch of sea salt

**1** Toss the parsnips with oil, garlic, thyme sprigs and sea salt and place in a roasting pan. Bake in a preheated oven, 200°C (400°F), Gas Mark 6, for 40-45 minutes, stirring occasionally until golden and tender.
**2** Meanwhile, melt the butter in a small pan and fry the thyme, lemon and cayenne over a gentle heat for 2-3 minutes until softened. Leave to infuse while the parsnips cook.
**3** Remove the parsnips from the oven, discard the thyme sprigs and dot over the thyme butter. Toss well and serve at once.

**Serves 4**
Preparation time: 10 minutes
Cooking time: 40-45 minutes
Oven temperature: 200°C (400°F), Gas Mark 6

# Baked Butternut Squash

*Serve this stuffed baked squash as a hearty supper dish, with a green salad.*

2 small butternut squash (about
    500 g/1 lb each)
3 tablespoons extra virgin olive oil
1 large onion, chopped finely
1 garlic clove, crushed
1 tablespoon chopped fresh thyme
1 teaspoon ground coriander
50 g/2 oz fresh wholemeal
    breadcrumbs
50 g/2 oz walnuts, toasted and
    chopped
50 g/2 oz drained sun-dried tomatoes
    in oil, chopped
2 tablespoons chopped fresh basil
200 g/7 oz firm vegetarian goats'
    cheese, cut thinly into 8 slices
salt and pepper

**1** Prick each butternut squash several times with a skewer and bake in a preheated oven, 190°C (375°F), Gas Mark 5, for 35-45 minutes. Remove the butternut squash from the oven and set aside until cool enough to handle.

**2** Meanwhile, heat half the oil in a frying pan, add the onion, garlic, thyme and coriander and fry gently for 10 minutes. Heat the remaining oil in a clean pan and stir-fry the breadcrumbs for 4-5 minutes until crisp and golden.

**3** Cut each squash in half lengthways and discard the seeds. Carefully scoop out the flesh and chop finely. Place the flesh in a bowl and stir in the onion mixture, breadcrumbs, walnuts, tomatoes and basil and season well.

**4** Divide the filling between the squash shells and arrange 3 slices of cheese over the top of each one. Return to the oven and bake for a further 30 minutes until tender.

**Serves 4**
Preparation time: 20 minutes
Cooking time: 1 hour 15 minutes
Oven temperature: 190°C (375°F),
Gas Mark 5

## Stir-fried Greens with Turnips

*Spring greens are available most of the year, but are naturally at their best during the spring months. There are several different varieties of greens, from simple spring greens to brussels sprouts tops, beetroot tops and even curly kale. Use small turnips as an alternative to baby turnips and put several different varieties of spring greens. Ordinary green cabbage can also be used instead of spring greens.*

500 g/1 lb spring greens
4 tablespoons extra virgin olive oil
175 g/6 oz baby turnips, sliced
4 tablespoons vegetable stock
1 teaspoon balsamic vinegar
2 garlic cloves, sliced
2 teaspoons grated lemon rind
50 g/2 oz raisins
40 g/1½ oz pine nuts, toasted

**1** Trim all the spring greens and discard the thick central stalk. Shred the spring greens thinly and blanch in a large pan of lightly salted, boiling water for 1 minute, then drain and refresh the greens under cold water and pat them dry on paper towels.
**2** Heat half the oil in a small frying pan and fry the turnips for 5 minutes until lightly golden. Add the stock and vinegar, cover and cook over a low heat for a further 3 minutes.
**3** Heat the remaining oil in a wok or large frying pan, add the garlic, lemon rind, raisins and pine nuts and stir-fry for 2 minutes. Add the spring greens, stir-fry for a further 5 minutes until the spring greens are tender and then stir in the turnips with their juices. Heat through and serve immediately.

**Serves 4**
Preparation time: 15 minutes
Cooking time: 20-23 minutes

## Melanzane Parmigiana

*This layered bake of aubergines and cheese is a classic Italian dish. I have used grated Cheddar rather than the more usual mozzarella – I find the texture is better and it has a richer flavour.*

**6 medium aubergines**
**salt**
**2 tablespoons extra virgin olive oil**
**1 quantity Fresh Tomato Sauce (see page 126)**
**250 g/8 oz vegetarian Cheddar cheese, grated**
**50 g/2 oz freshly grated vegetarian Parmesan cheese**

**1** Trim the aubergines and cut lengthways into thick slices. Sprinkle with salt and set aside to drain in a colander for 30 minutes. Wash well, drain and pat dry on paper towels.

**2** Brush the aubergine slices with oil and place on 2 large baking sheets. Roast the aubergines at the top of a preheated oven, 200°C (400°F), Gas Mark 6, for 10 minutes on each side until golden and tender.

**3** Meanwhile, reheat the tomato sauce and keep warm.

**4** Spoon a little of the tomato sauce into a lasagne dish and top with a layer of aubergines and some of the Cheddar cheese. Continue with the layers finishing with the Cheddar. Sprinkle over the Parmesan cheese and bake for 30 minutes until bubbling and golden. Serve hot with a crisp green salad and bread to mop up the juices.

**Serves 6**
Preparation time: 10 minutes, plus 30 minutes draining and making the sauce
Cooking time: 40 minutes, plus sauce
Oven temperature: 200°C (400°F), Gas Mark 6

## *Herb Roulade with Spinach Ricotta*

**25 g/1 oz butter**
**40 g/1½ oz plain flour**
**1 teaspoon Dijon mustard**
**200 ml/7 fl oz semi-skimmed milk**
**50 g/2 oz vegetarian cheese, grated**
**4 eggs, separated**
**4 tablespoons chopped mixed fresh**
   **herbs (basil, chervil, chives, tarragon,**
   **thyme)**

FILLING:

**175 g/6 oz ricotta or curd cheese**
**2 tablespoons extra virgin olive oil, plus**
   **extra for oiling**
**pinch of grated nutmeg**
**1 leek,  finely chopped**
**500 g/1 lb frozen leaf spinach,**
   **thawed, drained and squeezed**
**¼ teaspoon freshly grated nutmeg**
**salt and pepper**
**Fresh Tomato Sauce (see page 126), to**
   **serve**

**1** Grease and line a 23 x 33 cm/ 9 x 13 inch Swiss roll tin with baking parchment. Melt the butter in a pan, add the flour and mustard, cook over a low heat for 1 minute then gradually add the milk, stirring. Bring the sauce slowly to the boil, stirring constantly until the sauce thickens. Cook gently for 2 minutes.

**2** Remove the pan from the heat and cool slightly, Beat in the cheese, egg yolks, herbs and seasoning. Whisk the egg whites until stiff and fold into the sauce until evenly incorporated.

**3** Pour the mixture into the prepared tin and bake in a preheated oven, 200°C (400°F), Gas Mark 6, for 12-15 minutes until risen and firm to the touch. Remove from the oven and set aside to cool. Lower the temperature to 190°C (375°F), Gas Mark 5.

**4** Meanwhile, prepare the filling. Cream the cheese and half the oil together and season with nutmeg, salt and pepper.

**5** Heat the remaining oil in a frying pan and then fry the leeks for 5 minutes. Squeeze out all the water from the spinach, chop the spinach finely and add to the pan. Cook gently for 5 minutes.

**6** To assemble the roulade, turn out of the tin, carefully peel away the paper. Spread over the softened cheese and then the spinach mixture. Roll up from 1 short end and place on the oiled baking sheet. Brush with oil and bake for 20-25 minutes. Serve hot in slices, with fresh tomato sauce (see page 126).

**Serves 6**
Preparation time: 40 minutes, plus making sauce
Cooking time: 40-50 minutes
Oven temperature: 200°C (400°F), Gas Mark 6, then 190°C (375°F), Gas Mark 5

## Cabbage and Caraway Gratin

50 g/2 oz butter, plus extra for
   greasing
500 g/1 lb savoy cabbage, sliced
1 leek, trimmed, cleaned and
   sliced
2 teaspoons caraway seeds
2 tablespoons wholegrain mustard
50 g/2 oz fresh breadcrumbs
50 g/2 oz walnut pieces, chopped
175 g/6 oz Gruyère or vegetarian
   Cheddar cheese, grated
salt and pepper

**1** Melt half the butter in a frying pan and fry the savoy cabbage, leek and caraway seeds for 15 minutes until the cabbage is just tender. Stir in the wholegrain mustard.

**2** Melt the remaining butter and fry the breadcrumbs and walnuts for 5 minutes until lightly golden. Stir into the cabbage and season well.

**3** Layer the cabbage mixture with the cheese into 1 large or 6 shallow greased baking dishes, finishing the layering with a layer of cheese. Cover with foil and bake in a preheated oven, 200°C (400°F), Gas Mark 6, for 20 minutes until the cabbage is tender to the bite. Brown the gratin under a hot grill and serve immediately.

**Serves 6**
Preparation time: 15 minutes
Cooking time: 40 minutes
Oven temperature: 200°C (425°F),
Gas Mark 6

# Cauliflower Ginger and Saffron Frittata

*A frittata is an Italian set omelette usually served warm or cold. The saffron adds a hint of the exotic and combines particularly well with the cauliflower. I think this particular frittata is best served hot, straight from the pan.*

4 tablespoons milk
¼ teaspoon saffron threads
1 teaspoon sesame oil
8 large eggs (size 1), beaten
½ teaspoon salt
2 tablespoons chopped fresh coriander

2 tablespoons vegetable oil
1 leek, trimmed, cleaned and sliced
1 tablespoon grated root ginger
1 small cauliflower (about 450 g/
    12 oz) divided into small florets
1 tablespoon sesame seeds

**1** Warm the milk and saffron threads in a small saucepan until almost boiling, remove from the heat, add the sesame oil and set aside for 10 minutes to infuse. Beat in the eggs, salt and coriander.
**2** Heat the vegetable oil in a large heavy-bottomed non-stick frying pan. Add the leek, ginger and cauliflower and fry over a medium heat for 10 minutes until lightly golden.
**3** Stir in the egg mixture until evenly combined and cook over a medium heat for 8-10 minutes until the frittata is almost set. Sprinkle over the sesame seeds.
**4** Place the pan under a preheated grill and cook for 3-4 minutes until browned. Cool slightly, carefully remove the frittata from the pan, cut into wedges and serve hot.

**Serves 4**
Preparation time: 12 minutes, plus infusing time
Cooking time: 25 minutes

VARIATION

# Potato, Red Onion and Feta Tortilla

4 tablespoons extra virgin olive oil
1 red onion, sliced
2 garlic cloves, crushed
1 red chilli, deseeded and chopped
2 medium potatoes, diced
8 eggs
2 tablespoons chopped fresh parsley
125 g/4 oz vegetarian feta cheese,
    diced
salt and pepper

**1** Heat 3 tablespoons of the oil in a frying pan, add the onion, garlic and chilli and fry for 5 minutes. Add the potato and cook for a further 10 minutes, stirring occasionally. Remove from the heat and cool slightly.
**2** Beat the eggs with the remaining ingredients and stir in the cooled potato mixture. Set aside for 30 minutes for the flavours to infuse.
**3** Heat the remaining oil in a non-stick frying pan, add the egg mixture and cook for 8 minutes or until just set through. Transfer to a hot grill and cook for 3-4 minutes until set and browned on the top.
**4** Cool in the pan for 10 minutes. Turn out and leave to cool to room temperature, cut in wedges to serve.

**Serves 4-6**
Preparation time: 10 minutes, plus 30 minutes infusing
Cooking time: 25-30 minutes

# Breakfast Gratin

4 tablespoons extra virgin olive oil
175 g/6 oz button mushrooms,
    quartered if large
1 onion, roughly chopped
4 small cooked potatoes, cubed
4 small tomatoes, halved
4 small eggs (size 5)
125 g/4 oz vegetarian Cheddar
    cheese, grated
2 tablespoons chopped fresh chives or
    parsley
salt and pepper

**1** Heat half the oil in a large frying
pan or skillet, add the mushrooms
and onion and fry for 5 minutes until
golden. Remove with a slotted spoon
and set aside. Add the remaining oil
and fry the potatoes for 5-6 minutes
until golden.
**2** Increase the heat, stir in the tomatoes and fry over a high heat for
2-3 minutes until lightly golden. Return
the mushrooms and onions to the pan.
**3** Make 4 holes in the mixture and
carefully break an egg into each
hole. Scatter over the cheese and
place under a hot grill for 4-5 minutes until the eggs are set and the
cheese bubbling and golden.
**4** Sprinkle over the chopped chives
or parsley and serve at once with
toasted bread.

**Serves 4**
Preparation time: 15 minutes
Cooking time: 18-20 minutes

# Baked Spring Green and Potato 'Cake'

*Serve this baked mashed potato dish as an accompaniment to a hearty stew such as the Speedy Mixed Baked Beans (see page 57). It is also tasty served on its own with Mushroom Gravy (see page 127) as an easy mid-week supper dish.*

500 g/1 lb potatoes
250 g/8 oz green peas, thawed if frozen
250 g/8 oz spring greens
4 eggs, lightly beaten
2 garlic cloves, crushed
2 tablespoons chopped fresh mint
1 tablespoon wholegrain mustard
25 g/1 oz fresh breadcrumbs
25 g/1 oz freshly grated vegetarian Parmesan cheese
vegetable oil, for oiling
15 g/½ oz flaked almonds
salt

**1** Cook the potatoes for 15-20 minutes until tender. Meanwhile cook the peas for 8-10 minutes until tender. Drain both and press through a vegetable mouli or mash well together.
**2** Trim the greens, discarding the thick central stalk. Chop roughly and blanch in salted boiling water for 1 minute, drain well and dry. Mix into the mashed potato and peas.

**3** Gradually beat the eggs into the vegetable mixture and then stir in garlic, mint and mustard. Combine the breadcrumbs and Parmesan.
**4** Oil a 20 x 30 cm/8 x 12 inch baking dish and line with half the breadcrumb mixture. Pour in the potato mixture and top with the remaining breadcrumbs and finally the almonds. Bake in a preheated oven, 180°C (350°F), Gas Mark 4, for 40 minutes until puffed and lightly golden and the centre is firm. Leave to sit for 5 minutes before serving.

**Serve 8**
Preparation time: 25 minutes
Cooking time: 1 hour, plus 5 minutes resting time
Oven temperature: 180°C (350°F), Gas Mark 4

## Asparagus and Broad Bean Omelette

*This is a fresh tasting omelette best made in the early summer when both vegetables are in season. Although time consuming, broad beans are much nicer when the tough outer skin of the bean is removed. The inner bean is tender and succulent, and a vivid green.*

125 g/4 oz asparagus
125 g/4 oz podded broad beans,
  thawed if frozen
40 g/1½ oz butter or vegetable
  margarine

6 large eggs (size 1)
2 tablespoons milk
2 tablespoons chopped fresh chervil or
  dill
salt and pepper

**1** Trim the asparagus spears and cut into 5 cm/2 inch lengths and then in half lengthways. Blanch the broad beans in boiling water for 1 minute, then drain. Remove the tough outer skin of the beans.
**2** Melt 15 g/½ oz of the butter or margarine in a frying pan, add the vegetables and fry for 2-3 minutes. Cover the pan and cook for a further 3-4 minutes until just tender.
**3** Lightly whisk the eggs with the milk, chervil or dill and plenty of salt and pepper, until just combined. Heat a large non-stick frying pan, add the remaining butter and heat until the butter starts to foam.
**4** Add the eggs and stir gently, using a wooden spatula, drawing the mixture in from the sides of the pan as it starts to set. When the eggs have almost set, leave to cook for a further minute to brown the underneath.
**5** Spoon the asparagus and broad beans on to one half of the omelette. Tip the pan away from you and using, a palette knife, carefully fold the omelette over to almost enclose the filling. Slide the omelette on to a warmed plate and serve at once.

**Serves 2**
Preparation time: 15 minutes
Cooking time: 12-15 minutes

VARIATION

## Omelette with Cherry Tomatoes and Chopped Herbs

3 tablespoons extra virgin olive oil
125 g/4 oz cherry tomatoes, halved
2 tablespoons chopped fresh herbs
  (basil, chervil, chives, mint, tarragon,
  thyme)
1 teaspoon grated lemon rind
3 eggs, beaten
1 tablespoon Red Pesto (see page 126)
2 tablespoons milk
salt and pepper

**1** Heat 2 tablespoons of the oil in a small frying pan and fry the tomatoes, herbs and lemon rind for 3 minutes until the tomatoes start to soften. Remove from the heat and keep warm.
**2** Heat the remaining oil in an omelette pan. Beat the eggs, pesto, milk and salt and pepper together, then swirl into the pan. Cook gently for 3-4 minutes until almost set. Spoon on the tomato mixture, flip over the omelette, cook for a further 1 minute and slip on to a warmed serving plate.

**Serves 1-2**
Preparation time: 5 minutes, plus making pesto
Cooking time: 8 minutes

## Basic Pancakes

*This recipe is suitable for both savoury and sweet pancakes. They freeze well, and can be kept warm for up to 30 minutes: stack on a plate, cover with clingfilm, and place over a pan of gently simmering water.*

125 g/4 oz plain flour
pinch of salt
1 egg, lightly beaten
300 ml/½ pint milk
vegetable oil, for frying

**1** Sift the flour and salt into a bowl and make a well in the middle. Gradually beat in the egg and then the milk to form a smooth batter with a thick pouring consistency. Cover and leave to rest for 20 minutes.
**2** Using an omelette pan or small flat frying pan, about 18 cm/7 inch in diameter, brush the surface of the pan with a little oil and heat until just starting to smoke.
**3** Take a ladleful of the batter, pour on to the pan and swirl the mixture to cover the base in a thin even layer. Cook for 2-3 minutes until browned

underneath, flip over with a palette knife and cook the other side for a further 1-2 minutes until browned. Remove from the pan and repeat with the remaining batter to make 8 pancakes, brushing the pan with a little oil before adding the next spoonful of batter.

**Serves 4**
Preparation time: 5 minutes, plus 20 minutes resting
Cooking time: 3-5 minutes per pancake

**VARIATIONS**

## Herb pancakes

Add 4 tablespoons chopped fresh herbs to the pancake batter; choose your favourite herbs.

## Buckwheat pancakes

Replace half the plain flour with an equal amount of buckwheat flour.

## Spinach pancakes

Drain 125 g/4 oz thawed frozen spinach and squeeze out excess liquid. Chop finely and beat into the batter with the milk.

# Spinach Pancake and Asparagus Gratin

**24 thick asparagus stalks**
**8 Spinach Pancakes (see left)**
**vegetable oil, for oiling**
**½ quantity Classic White Sauce (see page 127)**
**50 g/2 oz vegetarian Cheshire cheese, grated**

**1** Trim the asparagus stalks and blanch in a large pan of lightly salted, boiling water for 2 minutes. Drain, refresh under cold water and pat dry on paper towels.

**2** Place 3 asparagus stalks on each pancake and roll up. Place each pancake seam-side down in an oiled baking dish.

**3** Pour over the white sauce and scatter over the cheese. Place under a medium grill and cook for 8-10 minutes until bubbling and golden. Serve at once.

**Serves 4**
Preparation time: 5 minutes, plus making pancakes and sauce
Cooking time: 12-15 minutes, plus pancakes and sauce

## Rhubarb, Apple and Double Ginger Crumble

*Both ginger biscuits and preserved stem ginger are added to this crumble to make it a little bit special.*

125 g/4 oz plain flour
50 g/2 oz ginger biscuits, ground
25 g/1 oz porridge oats
75 g/3 oz unsalted butter, plus extra for greasing
3 tablespoons light muscavado sugar

FILLING:

500 g/1 lb rhubarb, chopped
2 tablespoons chopped preserved stem ginger
2 tablespoons ginger syrup from jar
50 g/2 oz caster sugar
4 tablespoons water
375 g/12 oz dessert apples, peeled, cored and sliced
15 g/½ oz unsalted butter

**1** Sift the flour into a bowl and stir in the ground ginger biscuits and oats. Rub in the butter until the mixture resembles breadcrumbs and stir in the sugar.
**2** Place the rhubarb in a saucepan with the chopped ginger, ginger syrup, sugar and water. Heat gently, cover and simmer for 10 minutes.
**3** Place the sliced apples in a greased pie dish. Add the rhubarb and butter and sprinkle over the crumble topping.
**4** Bake in a preheated oven, 190°C (375°F), Gas Mark 5, for 40 minutes until bubbling and the topping is golden. Serve the crumble hot with crème fraîche or fromage frais.

**Serves 8**
Preparation time: 20 minutes
Cooking time: 50 minutes
Oven temperature: 190°C (375°F), Gas Mark 5

# Warm Expresso Chocolate Pots

*Use a good quality dark chocolate with a high percentage of cocoa butter - at least 75%.*

**175 g/6 oz dark chocolate, chopped**
**250 ml/8 fl oz strong expresso coffee**
**2 tablespoons whisky**
**50 g/2 oz sugar**
**6 egg yolks**
**50 ml/2 fl oz double cream**
**grated nutmeg**

**1** Place the chocolate in a small pan with the coffee, whisky and heat gently until the chocolate has melted. Add the sugar and stir until dissolved. Remove from the heat.
**2** Immediately beat in the egg yolks until thickened. Pour through a fine sieve into 8 small expresso cups or ramekins. Cool and chill for 4 hours or overnight until set.
**3** Whip the cream until it just holds its shape and spoon a little on to each chocolate pot. Sprinkle with nutmeg. Pour a small amount of boiling water into a roasting dish to a depth of about 1 cm/½ inch. Sit the chocolate pots in the boiling water for 1 minute, then remove and serve immediately.

**Serves 8**
Preparation time: 5 minutes
Cooking time: 5 minutes, plus cooling and setting

## Strawberry and Lychee Sorbet

*A very light refreshing sorbet - the lychee flavour comes through just after the strawberry flavour.*

1 x 400 g/14 oz can lychees in light syrup
175 g/6 oz caster sugar
120 ml/4 fl oz water
750 g/1½ lb strawberries, hulled
1 tablespoon lemon juice

**1** Strain the lychee juice into a saucepan. Halve the lychees, cut away any brown shell that remains and add the flesh to the pan. Heat gently for 5 minutes and then process in a blender until fairly smooth.
**2** Put the sugar and water in a clean pan and heat gently until the sugar is dissolved. Bring to the boil and simmer for 3 minutes. Remove from the heat and allow to cool.
**3** Process the hulled strawberries in a blender with the lemon juice, add the cooled sugar and water syrup as you blend. Pass through a sieve to

remove pips and stir into the lychees.
**4** Transfer the mixture to a plastic container and freeze for 1 hour. Remove from the freezer, beat the mixture to break up any ice crystals and freeze for a further hour. Repeat the beating and freezing once again and then freeze until firm.
**5** Remove the sorbet from the freezer about 15 minutes before serving, to soften slightly, and serve in scoops.

**Serves 4**
Preparation time: 15 minutes
Cooking time: 15 minutes, plus freezing

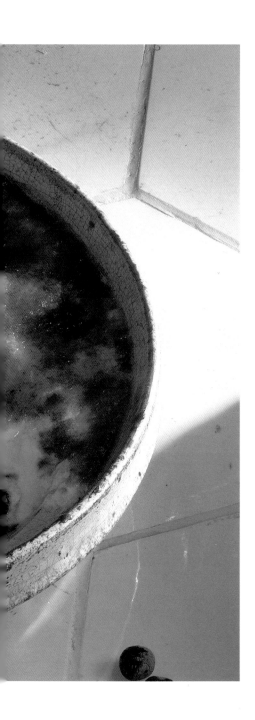

# Peach, Apricot and Blueberry Gratin

*A quick and simple dessert best made when fresh apricots and peaches are in season. American blueberries are available most of the year, or raspberries make a good substitute.*

4 firm ripe peaches, halved, stoned
    and very thinly sliced
6 firm ripe apricots, halved, stoned
    and very thinly sliced
175 g/6 oz blueberries

250 g/8 oz mascarpone cheese
250 g/8 oz Greek yogurt
3 tablespoons light muscavado sugar
1 teaspoon ground cinnamon

**1** Spoon the peaches and apricots into a gratin dish with the blueberries.
**2** Beat the mascarpone and yogurt together and spread over the fruit.
**3** Combine the sugar and cinnamon, sprinkle over the gratin to cover the surface and cook under a hot grill for 5-6 minutes until the sugar is caramelized. Cool for a few minutes and serve.

**Serves 6**
Preparation time: 10 minutes
Cooking time: 5-6 minutes

**VARIATION**

# Amaretti Fruit Gratin

Crumble 125 g/4 oz amaretti biscuits in the bottom of the gratin dish, add the fruit and 4 tablespoons Kirsch and cook as above.

## Exotic Melon and Rosewater Salad

*Exotic fruits and rosewater make a delicious fruit salad.*

**2 small Charantais melons**
**1 large ripe mango**
**1 large ripe papaya**
**2 tablespoons lime juice**
**4 tablespoons rosewater**
**1 tablespoon chopped fresh lemon balm**
**1 tablespoon pistachio nuts, chopped**
**rose petals, to decorate (optional)**

**1** Cut the melons in half, and scoop out and discard the seeds, holding the melons over a sieve set over a large bowl, to catch all the juices. Using a melon baller scoop out the flesh and place in a bowl.

**2** Cut the mango down each side of the central stone, and peel and cut the flesh into small cubes. Halve the papaya, scoop out and discard the seeds, peel and dice the flesh. Add the mango and papaya to the melon balls in the bowl.

**3** Mix the lime juice and rosewater together, pour over the fruit and chill for 1 hour. Stir in the lemon balm.

Spoon the fruit mixture into the hollow melon shells, sprinkle over the nuts, decorate with the rose petals and serve at once.

**Serves 4**
Preparation time: 15 minutes
Chilling time: 1 hour

# Banana Filo Pie

*Baked bananas are just about my favourite food and here they make a lovely gooey filling for filo pastry.*

50 g/2 oz unsalted butter
8 large sheets filo pastry, thawed if
   frozen
3 firm ripe bananas
25 g/1 oz sultanas
15 g/½ oz soft brown sugar
1 tablespoon dark rum
1 teaspoon grated lemon rind
25 g/1 oz flaked almonds, toasted
icing sugar, for dusting

**1** Melt 40 g/1½ oz of the butter in a small saucepan. Separate the pastry into sheets. Brush 1 sheet of pastry with the melted butter and top with a second sheet of pastry, brush with butter and repeat twice. Keep the remaining pastry sheets covered with a damp tea towel to prevent them drying out.
**2** Peel and thinly slice the bananas and arrange in a 23 cm/9 inch circle in the centre of the pastry. Top the bananas with the sultanas, sugar, rum, lemon rind and almonds and then dot with the remaining butter.
**3** Place the remaining sheets of pastry over the top of the pie, brush each sheet of pastry with melted butter and press firmly down around the filling. Using a fluted flan ring or plate cut around the pie, be sure to leave a 1 cm/½ inch edge.

**4** Brush over the remaining melted butter and bake in a preheated oven, 190°C (375°F), Gas Mark 5, for 25-30 minutes. Allow the pie to cool slightly and serve dusted with icing sugar.

**Serves 6**
Preparation time: 20 minutes
Cooking time: 30-35 minutes
Oven temperature: 190°C (375°F),
Gas Mark 5

# Poached Figs in Cassis with Cinnamon Sauce

*I have found fresh figs such a disappointment when they appear in the shops – nothing compared to those I've enjoyed abroad. However, this method of poaching them in a cassis and red wine syrup seems to be a great success.*

300 ml/½ pint red wine
150 ml/¼ pint cassis
2 cinnamon sticks
2 strips lemon peel
2 strips orange peel
300 ml/½ pint water
12 large firm ripe figs, washed

SAUCE:
150 g/5 oz Greek yogurt
2 tablespoons Greek honey
1 teaspoon ground cinnamon

**1** Place the wine, cassis, cinnamon sticks, citrus peel and water in a saucepan and bring to the boil.
**2** Add the figs, cover the pan and simmer gently for 10 minutes until the figs are dark red and softened. Do not over-cook or the figs will fall apart.
**3** Remove the figs with a slotted spoon and place in a serving dish. Bring the poaching liquid to a rolling boil and simmer until it is reduced by half and is thick and syrupy. Pour over the figs and leave to cool.
**5** Meanwhile, combine all the sauce ingredients together and set aside for the flavours to develop. Serve the figs at room temperature with a spoonful of sauce for each serving.

**Serves 4**
Preparation time: 10 minutes, plus chilling time
Cooking time: 10 minutes

VARIATION

# Poached Pears

Replace the 12 figs with 6 firm, ripe pears. Peel the pears and cook them in the syrup for about 40 minutes until cooked through but not mushy. Remove the pears from the syrup and continue as left.

# Filo Horns with Mixed Berries and Raspberry Sauce

6 large sheets filo pastry, thawed if frozen
75 g/3 oz unsalted butter, melted, plus extra for greasing
175 g/6 oz ricotta or curd cheese
1 tablespoon clear honey
25 g/1 oz ground almonds, toasted
625 g/1¼ lb mixed summer berries
SAUCE:
250 g/8 oz frozen raspberries, thawed
2 tablespoons Grand Marnier (optional)
3 tablespoons icing sugar, plus extra for dusting
toasted flaked almonds, to decorate

**1** Cut each sheet of pastry into 2 x 15 cm/6 inch squares, brush each square with butter and fold in half diagonally to form 12 triangles. Wrap 1 triangle around each greased cream horn mould, brush with the remaining butter and place on a large greased baking sheet, seam-side down.

**2** Bake the filo horns in a preheated oven, 190°C (375°F), Gas Mark 5, for 15 minutes until crisp and golden. Leave to cool before carefully extracting the pastry from the horn moulds.

**3** Beat together the ricotta or curd cheese, honey and almonds. Hull and slice the fruits as necessary.

**4** Make the sauce. Place the raspberries in a blender and process until smooth. Pass through a fine sieve to remove the pips and whisk in the Grand Marnier, if using, and the icing sugar.

**5** Just before serving, pipe the ricotta mixture into the filo horns to come two-thirds of the way to the top. Pile in the fruits and serve 2 horns per person with the raspberry sauce. Dust with sifted icing sugar and scatter over the toasted flaked almonds.

**Serves 6**
Preparation time: 40 minutes
Cooking time: 15 minutes
Oven temperature: 190°C (375°F), Gas Mark 5

12 bay leaves, bruised
2 tablespoons lemon rind
150 ml/¼ pint double cream
4 eggs
1 egg yolk
150 g/5 oz caster sugar
100 ml/3½ fl oz lemon juice

**1** Put the bay leaves, lemon rind and cream in a small saucepan and heat gently until it reaches boiling point. Remove from the heat and set aside for 2 hours to infuse.
**2** Whisk the eggs, egg yolk and sugar together until the mixture is pale and creamy and then whisk in the lemon juice. Strain the cream mixture through a fine sieve into the bowl and stir until combined.
**3** Pour the custard equally into 8 individual ramekin dishes and place on a baking sheet. Bake in a preheated oven, 125°C (225°F), Gas Mark ½ for 50 minutes or until the custards are almost set in the middle. Leave to go cold and chill until required. Return to room temperature before serving.

**Serves 8**
Preparation time: 5 minutes, plus
2 hours infusing
Cooking time: 55-60 minutes
Oven temperature: 125°C (225°F),
Gas Mark ½

## Baked Lemon and Bay Custards

*This recipe is a variation of the old classic lemon tart. Here, the lemon custard is also infused with bay leaves, giving it a heady scent. The custard is poured into ramekin dishes and baked in a very low oven: if the oven is too hot the custard will curdle. Check after 40 minutes - the centres should be almost set but still move a little - they will firm up as they cool.*

# STOCKS AND SAUCES

## Vegetable Stock

4 tablespoons sunflower oil
2 whole garlic cloves
2 onions, chopped roughly
2 leeks, trimmed, cleaned and sliced
4 carrots, chopped
2 medium potatoes, diced
4 celery sticks, sliced
4 ripe tomatoes, chopped roughly
125 g/4 oz mushrooms, wiped
125 g/4 oz rice
1 bouquet garni (see page 8)
1.75 litres/3 pints water

**1** Heat the oil in a large saucepan, add the garlic, onions and leeks and fry gently for 10 minutes until light golden. Add the carrots, potatoes and celery and fry for a further 10 minutes.
**2** Add the remaining ingredients, bring to the boil, cover and simmer gently for 30 minutes. Strain the stock through a fine sieve and use as required or reduce to the required quantity.

**Makes 1.5 litres/2½ pints before reduction**
Preparation time: 15 minutes
Cooking time: 40 minutes

## Fresh Tomato Sauce

1 kg/2 lb ripe tomatoes, chopped roughly
2 tablespoons extra virgin olive oil
2 garlic cloves, chopped
2 tablespoons chopped fresh basil
1 teaspoon grated lemon rind
pinch of sugar
salt and pepper

**1** Place all the ingredients in a saucepan and bring to the boil. Cover and simmer over a gentle heat for 30 minutes.
**2** Remove the lid and cook for 20 minutes until the sauce is thick. Adjust seasonings. Use as required.

**Makes approximately 600 ml/1 pint**
Preparation time: 10 minutes
Cooking time: 50 minutes

**VARIATION**

## Quick Tomato Sauce

Use 2 x 400 g/14 oz cans chopped tomatoes. Cook as above, but simmer for 10 minutes only.

## Pesto Sauce

*This wonderfully fragrant sauce is a fundamental part of Italian cuisine.*

1 garlic clove, crushed
25 g/1 oz pine nuts
25 g/1 oz basil leaves
75 ml (3 fl oz) extra virgin olive oil
2 tablespoons freshly grated
   vegetarian Parmesan cheese
salt and pepper

**1** Place the garlic, pine nuts and basil in a blender and process until fairly smooth (or grind using a pestle and mortar). Gradually beat in the oil, then stir in the cheese and adjust seasoning.

**Makes about 150 ml/¼ pint**
Preparation time: 10 minutes

**VARIATION**

## Red Pesto

Add 50 g/2 oz drained and sliced sun-dried tomatoes in oil to the above ingredients and blend to a rough paste. You can also substitute half the oil from the jar for half the olive oil for an even stronger flavour.

# Mushroom Gravy

15 g/½ oz dried ceps
300 ml/½ pint boiling water
25 g/1 oz butter
4 shallots, chopped
500 g/1 lb field mushrooms, sliced
2 tablespoons plain flour
150 ml/¼ pint dry sherry or white wine
4 thyme sprigs
4 rosemary sprigs
600 ~¹/1 pint Vegetable Stock (see page 126)
salt and pepper

**1** Soak the dried ceps in the boiling water for 30 minutes then strain, reserving the liquid. Slice the ceps.
**2** Melt the butter in a saucepan and fry the shallots for 5 minutes. Add the mushrooms and ceps and fry for a further 5 minutes until the mushrooms are tender.
**3** Stir in the flour and cook for 1 minute. Gradually whisk in the sherry or wine and cep liquid and boil for 5 minutes. Strain through a fine sieve into a clean pan.
**4** Add the herbs and stock, bring to the boil and boil rapidly for 10-15 minutes until reduced by half. Season to taste, strain and serve at once.

**Makes approximately 400 ml/14 fl oz**
Preparation time: 10 minutes, plus 30 minutes soaking
Cooking time: 20-25 minutes

# Classic Mayonnaise

*I am a true believer in learning the basic cooking methods in the traditional manner then, once mastered, any relevant mod cons can be used, see below.*

1 egg yolk
2 teaspoons lemon juice
1 teaspoon Dijon mustard
pinch of sugar
salt and pepper
250-300 ml/8-10 fl oz extra virgin olive oil

**1** In a bowl whisk together the egg yolk, lemon juice, mustard, sugar and salt and pepper until pale and creamy.
**2** Gradually whisk in the oil, a little at a time, beating well after each addition until thick and pale. Add a little boiling water if the mixture is too thick. Taste and adjust seasonings.

**Makes approximately 300 ml/½ pint**
Preparation time: 5 minutes

### FOOD PROCESSOR VARIATION
Place the egg yolk, lemon juice, mustard, sugar and salt in a food processor and blend for 30 seconds until pale. With the blade running, add the oil in a steady stream through the funnel, until the sauce is thick and glossy. Thin with a little boiling water, if necessary.

# Classic White Sauce (Béchamel)

600 ml/1 pint milk
1 small onion, chopped roughly
1 bay leaf
50 g/2 oz butter
50 g/2 oz plain flour
1 teaspoon mustard powder
salt and pepper

**1** Put the milk, onion and bay leaf in a saucepan, heat gently until just boiling. Remove pan from the heat, set aside for 20 minutes so flavours infuse. Strain the milk and set aside.
**2** Melt the butter in a pan, stir in the flour and cook over a gentle heat for 1 minute. Remove from the heat and gradually beat in the infused milk a little at a time until evenly blended. Return to a low heat and stir constantly until the sauce thickens. Bring to a gentle boil, still stirring and simmer for 2 minutes.

**Makes approximately 600 ml/1 pint**
Preparation time: 5 minutes, plus 20 minutes infusing
Cooking time: 8-10 minutes

### VARIATION

## Rich Béchamel
Add 2 thyme sprigs and 2 parsley sprigs to 450 ml/¾ pint milk and 150 ml/¼ pint single cream. Heat together with the onion and bay leaf and continue as above.